to BELONG HERE

to BELONG HERE

A NEW GENERATION OF QUEER, TRANS, AND TWO-SPIRIT APPALACHIAN WRITERS

edited by **RAE GARRINGER**
founder of Country Queers

FOREWORD BY CARTER SICKELS

UNIVERSITY PRESS OF KENTUCKY

A note to the reader: This volume contains references to suicide and other sensitive topics, including oppression of and violence against members of the LGBTQ+ community and communities of color. Racist and homophobic slurs are reproduced here to accurately portray the experiences of the authors and their informants. Discretion is advised.

Copyright © 2025 by The University Press of Kentucky

Scholarly publisher for the Commonwealth, serving Bellarmine University, Berea College, Centre College of Kentucky, Eastern Kentucky University, The Filson Historical Society, Georgetown College, Kentucky Historical Society, Kentucky State University, Morehead State University, Murray State University, Northern Kentucky University, Spalding University, Transylvania University, University of Kentucky, University of Louisville, University of Pikeville, and Western Kentucky University. All rights reserved.

Editorial and Sales Offices: The University Press of Kentucky
663 South Limestone Street, Lexington, Kentucky 40508-4008
www.kentuckypress.com

Cataloging-in-Publication data is available from the Library of Congress.

ISBN 978-1-9859-0182-7 (hardcover : alk. paper)
ISBN 978-1-9859-0183-4 (paperback : alk. paper)
ISBN 978-1-9859-0184-1 (epub)
ISBN 978-1-9859-0185-8 (pdf)

This book is printed on acid-free paper meeting
the requirements of the American National Standard
for Permanence in Paper for Printed Library Materials.

Manufactured in the United States of America.

Member of the Association
of University Presses

for STAY
past, present, and future

Contents

Carter Sickels
Foreword   ix

Rae Garringer
Preface   xiii

Joy Cedar
Sanctuary   1

Brandon Sun Eagle Jent
What You Should Know Before You Kill Me   2

Rayna Momen
They Say All Kinds Are Welcome Here   4

Lucien Darjeun Meadows
Where Are You From?   5

Joy Cedar
School Eraser   16

hermelinda cortés
Volver, Volver   18

Rayna Momen
Growing Up Black in Appalachia   25

Joe Tolbert Jr.
To Repel Ghosts   27

Joy Cedar
Copperhead   36

Rae Garringer
Proximity   38

Brandon Sun Eagle Jent
Circles/Dances   48

Rayna Momen
Dear West Virginia   50

Jai Arun Ravine
What Anchors You Here   52

Brandon Sun Eagle Jent
Kentucky Waltz   61

G. Samantha Rosenthal
A Queer Place Called Home   63

Lauren Garretson-Atkinson
An Inheritance   71

Pumpkin Starr
4 lil poems on 4 big feelins   73

D. Stump
Prayers to a Greater Belonging   76

Brandon Sun Eagle Jent
this world loves me too   83

Acknowledgments   85
Contributors   87

Foreword

The first time I attended the Appalachian Writers' Workshop was in 2016, a month after the Pulse massacre and just a few months before the country decided to elect Donald Trump as president. The writers' workshop takes place at the Hindman Settlement School in the mountains of eastern Kentucky, and it's a kind of spiritual homecoming for writers who are from or living in Appalachia. Rae Garringer was a student in my fiction writing workshop that year, and we had many honest and compelling conversations about queer existence in rural places, Appalachia, and community.

On the last night of the five-day workshop, participants wandered up to the *Chapel in the Trees*, an open-air chapel built next to the graves of beloved Appalachian author James Still and settlement school cofounder May Stone. Fiddles and banjos and guitars were unpacked from cases, and soon, a range of voices joined the strings. Old-time music, bluegrass, and hymns lifted above the tops of the sycamores and oaks and out across the land, joining the pure notes of crickets and other night bugs. Jars of homemade moonshine and bottles of bourbon touched lips, passed hands. We were members of a wild church of poets and musicians and tall trees reaching toward starry skies. It was a hot, sweaty summer night, joyous and full. I don't remember the song we danced to, but Rae and I—two of only a handful of queers—found each other and two-stepped across the old stone floor. Rae led; I did my best to follow. We twirled and spun in this safe space, where we could be country and queer and not feel afraid.

In the years that followed, Rae and I developed a friendship, and I often turn to their work—the documentation of rural queer and trans experiences—for my own writing and to share with my queer and Appalachian students as we search for representation. Rae started the oral history project *Country Queers* in 2013 (which grew into a remarkable podcast of the same title) by driving all over the United States to connect with queer people surviving and thriving in rural places. As a queer trans man from rural America, I was hungry to hear these kinds of stories. I grew up in a small town in Ohio. For much of my life, the only stories I knew about queers in rural places ended in two ways. The first is a story of violence, as exemplified by *Brokeback Mountain*: cowboys may find queer love, but they can't survive. The second is a story of exodus: in order to find community and acceptance, in order to stay alive, queer and trans people must flee to big cities. These stories are not entirely wrong. Many queer people experience some form of violence—if not physical, then emotional—and have fled rural childhood homes for a more accepting urban existence, where it's easier to find queer community, health care, and work. I myself have spent most of my adult life in cities, including New York, Portland, Oregon, and now Durham, North Carolina. I often feel that, as a queer, trans man, I exist in a liminal space, between or beyond the gender binary, visible and invisible, and home is both elusive and expansive. In my fiction, I've tried to explore the complexity of home and queer lives in rural places, specifically in Appalachia.

I'm so pleased that Rae has continued their important work of creating an inclusive space for diverse queer and trans voices in *To Belong Here*, which focuses entirely on central Appalachia. This powerful collection of essays and poems gathers Black, Native, Latinx, Asian American, Indigenous, white, multiracial, queer, trans, and Two-Spirit authors who shatter the myth that Appalachia is a monolith of white, Christian, heterosexual, MAGA voters. The authors in this collection hold up the busted pieces of that myth to the light, turning them this way and that, and through their thoughtful words examine and illuminate the more complex and multiple truths about the region. Some of the writers in this collection grew up in cities or rural regions of Appalachia, a few arrived later, some fled, some stayed, some returned. They write of an uneasy love for Appalachia and the people who live here, and they don't romanticize or gloss over the more difficult realities. They name, explore, and interrogate the darker edges of Appalachia (which align with the darker edges of America): the violence of white supremacists, the political right-wing chokehold, the rampant toxic masculinity, the shameful history of the region's genocide and forced removal of Indigenous people, and the environmental devastation caused by strip mining and fracking. This collection makes space for the more nuanced, and sometimes messy and contradictory truths, about trans and queer identity and place. The authors wrestle with what it means to feel both deeply connected to and excluded from a place—to love a place that may not love you back—and examine the intersections of race, gender, sexuality, disability, and class.

If paying attention is a form of love, then it's clear these writers, even when it's difficult to do, love Appalachia, especially the natural world. They write with urgency, lyricism, and captivating details about the land, the trees and creeks, the gardens, the mountains, and the terrible loss and human-caused destruction. They ask urgent questions about survival: How can we practice stewardship of the land? How can we create sustainable and thoughtful community that honors the environment? The essays and poems in *To Belong Here* make visible the diverse, varied queer people living in Appalachia who are creating homes and communities and families and collective spaces.

Inherent in the dominant narratives of violence and exodus assigned to queer, rural, and Appalachian lives is the narrative of invisibility. I believe queer representation can save lives. *To Belong Here* shines a light on queer, trans, and Two-Spirit people living in, fleeing, and wrestling with the meanings of Appalachia, home, and rurality. These essays and poems tell profound and important stories of queer grief and joy, shame and survival, belonging and exile, visibility and possibility, community and the natural world. They examine the past and present with clear eyes, resist nostalgia and stereotypes, and reach for a bigger, more inclusive future: a place where two queer trans people can two-step and twirl under the stars on a summer night.

—**Carter Sickels** (he/him) is the author of the novel *The Prettiest Star*, winner of the Southern Book Prize and the Weatherford Award. His debut novel, *The Evening Hour*, an Oregon Book Award finalist and a Lambda Literary Award finalist, was adapted into a feature film that premiered at the 2020 Sundance Film Festival. His essays and fiction have appeared in a variety of publications, including *The Atlantic*, *Oxford American*, *Poets & Writers*, and *The Kenyon Review*. He is an assistant professor of English at North Carolina State University.

Preface

It is a blessing and a curse to love a place more than you love yourself. In 2011, I moved back home after nearly a decade away, and I told a friend that I felt like I'd been cheating on West Virginia by falling for all those boots and buckles, cacti and agave, sawdust-strewn dance floors and giant clouds over Texas. The first morning I woke up in the North Carolina piedmont, after reluctantly leaving West Virginia again in 2015 for graduate school, I felt my throat tighten before I even opened my eyes. I could feel the absence of these mountains in every inch of my body, even without sight.

I have never loved anything as much as I love southeastern West Virginia where I was raised. In some ways, it makes no sense. My family isn't from here. I don't only mean in the sense that I am the descendant of settlers on stolen Indigenous lands. I also mean that my family does not go back generations here. I wasn't even born here. We moved to West Virginia from the suburbs of Atlanta just weeks before my third birthday. Do I have a right to claim this place so strongly if I've spent a good ten years of my adult life living outside of the region? Do I have a right to write about this place as a transplant, even though it has been my home since my earliest memories?

The answer, of course, is yes. And also, I'd imagine, to some, it is no. Appalachia is nothing if not a place of conflicting narratives. There are tensions between the ways in which we see ourselves and the ways in which the national media portrays us. There are tensions between conflicting internal narratives of who and what belongs in and to this place, who really is *from* here, and where the boundaries of *here* even lie. From coalfields to farm fields, from the Chemical Valley to Pigeon Forge, from the Rust Belt of Pittsburgh to the coal ash dumps of Birmingham, from Knoxville to Hillsboro, there is no one Appalachian truth. There is no one Appalachian experience. There is no one Appalachia. I have no interest in even attempting to define it anymore, because I know that harsh and restrictive borders and binaries are killing us.

As the child of back-to-the-land hippies, educated in rural and often conservative West Virginia public schools, and then steeped in the radical left for twenty years, I know nothing better than what it feels like to live between multiple conflicting worlds simultaneously. I know the exhaustion that can emerge from not knowing how to make those disparate worlds fit together within your own body. I know the grief I feel when communities I love and inhabit see one another as enemies. And I know the relief that comes from spending time with others who also live with their limbs in many worlds, who also love these mountains deeply while wanting and needing so much here to change, and who are also navigating belonging to multiple communities that are often positioned as existing in opposition to one another.

I spent a decade traveling around rural parts of the continental United States, interviewing rural and small-town LGBTQIA2S+ folks for an oral history project I founded called *Country Queers*. I started that project in 2013 out of a deep personal need to meet and learn from other rural queer folks who knew how to live in a place like this, fully, bravely, unapologetically, and also respectfully to both ourselves and our neighbors. I learned a whole lot through meeting and listening to other rural queer folks all over, but I still have so many questions about how to do this: how to love a place that often hates you and your beloveds in return, how to love other queer and trans people outside these hills who think your neighbors and coworkers are their political enemies, how to defend a place while still pushing it forward, how to protect what's sacred, while atoning for past and present sins.

This book was born out of these questions and tensions. I wanted to know how other Appalachian based and/or raised queer, trans, and Two-Spirit people were navigating their own complicated, often contradictory, relationships to home and belonging in this region that we love so much but that often doesn't love us back. Not in all the ways we deserve to be loved at least. I wanted to explore some of the messiness of our lives in this region as queer, trans, and Two-Spirit people across multiple intersecting layers of identity including race, gender, and class. I wanted to explore some of the complexities of our experiences, which the page can hold in ways spoken conversations sometimes can't. I wanted to explore the deep internal tangles of how we make sense of our homes, of our places and bodies within them, of the harm they have caused us and others, the healing we find here too, and our ongoing love and commitment to them. I wanted to try to help create a book I wish already existed in the world—a collection of essays and poems by LGBTQIA2S+ central Appalachian writers that centers race and gender-expansiveness more concretely than previous collections on Appalachian sexuality have.

In my opinion, this book holds a dreamy combination of voices and brains, stories and memories. Several of the writers in this collection are friends who immediately came to mind when this book started to take shape in early conversations with Abby Freeland and Davis Shoulders at the University Press of Kentucky back in early 2021. Others are newer acquaintances, people who I only know so far through their words shared here, and this book is so much stronger because of their contributions. Others have become friends through the years it has taken for this collection to be born. Many of those included in this collection I first met through organizing spaces in the region. I have known that they were writers for years, but I also know well that many organizers aren't often able (or encouraged) to prioritize creative work amid these rapidly unfolding ongoing layers and cycles of crisis in our world. Many of those included in this collection have never, or rarely, been published before. I intentionally did not put out a public call for submissions for this collection, because I wanted to try to help foster a written space where writers in the region who likely would not respond to an open call for submissions would feel welcome. I wanted to encourage brilliant organizers to spend time with their creative voices. And I wanted to create an LGBTQIA2S+ collection in which writers of color, specifically Black and Indigenous writers, outnumbered white writers and in which trans and nonbinary writers outnumbered cis writers. In eight essays and thirteen poems by a gender-expansive multiracial group of writers living in, or hailing from, the central Appalachian region, this book digs into what it means to search for, long for, and even claim belonging in a place that often tries to run us off through settler colonialism, racist violence, transphobic legislation, suffocating religious conservatism, or straight up lack of opportunities and resources needed to survive, much less thrive.

These were not easy essays and poems to write. I sent dozens of emails back and forth and spent hours on the phone with some of these writers, trying to convince them that they do belong, not only in this collection but also in this place. I can say definitively that every writer within these pages struggled to dig into these questions of belonging in Appalachia. Multiple writers included in this book wrote to me at various points along the way, saying the process of exploring this theme was too raw, too painful, or too daunting to continue at the time. All of those writers, eventually, returned. I believe this collection is a necessary contribution to our regional conversations around race, gender, and sexuality, particularly in a political moment when legislative and violent physical attacks on the communities represented in this collection are rapidly and rabidly on the rise.

My hope for this book is that it deepens conversations and thinking around who truly *is* Appalachian and around who is given what Edward Said called "permission to narrate." My hope is that it pushes central Appalachian communities to engage in the work required to make this region a place where queer and trans people—and especially queer and trans people of color—can thrive. And I hope that it encourages readers outside these hills, who hold a million unconscious misconceptions about this place based on the stories they've heard in mainstream media, to approach this region with curiosity, with humility, and with an acknowledgment that the stories told about this place, both internally and externally, have long excluded so many of us.

It's past time for a more expansive and inclusive narrative around who exists, belongs, and deserves to thrive in this region and for a reality where, in the words of Ash-Lee Woodard Henderson, "everyone has everything they need."

Rae Garringer

Joy Cedar

Sanctuary

You don't have to believe me, but
These trees have known queer love so long
I wonder how many berry-blood-stained kisses they gave cover for
I like to think they rustled in celebration at love

Creator murmuring "Nudale udanto" *(they are different hearted)* when I was made
Were the trees asked to look after me?

I give thanks for the cedar,
the chokecherry,
the dogwood,
the oak

Who first taught you sanctuary?

Brandon Sun Eagle Jent

What You Should Know Before You Kill Me

Written with prayers of protection and peace for Two-Spirit, Indigiqueer, lesbian, gay, bisexual, trans, queer, intersex, asexual, and otherwise identified readers in Appalachia and beyond. For bubbies who are sissies and sissies who are bubbies. For those who defy definition.

Midsummer, noon. I answer your knock at the door and the wind rushes in, warm and sweet as sunbathed wildflowers. You cool my forehead with a barrel of gunmetal, finger just above the trigger, nose flaring with shallow breaths that reek of bloodlust. *Faggot, sissy, abomination*—these lost their edge long ago. Today, you come with a weapon sure to finish me off.

You wish me death? Which part of me? Every loose hair and shed tear, every nail clipping and nosebleed, the photons reflecting off every big-toothed smile, each wavelength in the birdsong of my raucous laughter, memories of me nesting inside the minds of those who have seen and known me, loved and hated me, understood me, were confused by me—will you find me there too? Will you kill me there too?

This body is but a wave in the ocean of me.

And where will the pain go? This pain that makes you writhe at the sight of me. Will your pain follow me through Death's gate, leave space for the peace you crave? I wish it were so simple. I used to want me dead, too. Yet we are children of the same earthen womb, kindred even when unclaimed.

Are you sure about this? This binding of bullet into breast and the sealing of our story: two strangers in a shotgun wedding, blood at first sight, marrying us forever into killer and killed, though death do us part. In an instance of mortal intimacy, you would be the last man I ever laid eyes on.

Can I at least know your name?

Before you make your decision, let's sit on the porch together. Let's lean back on trees transformed into rocking chairs, sip water and leaves I transformed into sweet tea, look at the seeds the rain transformed into flowers before you return me to the land that transformed into us.

In between sips, let your gun find its holster. Let me find my way back to the laundry. Let's leave the porch as white as eggshells, no need for fresh paint. After a couple deep breaths, leave your glass on the banister. Let the holler grow smaller in your rearview mirror; let it be your last sight of me.

Rayna Momen

They Say All Kinds Are Welcome Here

[unless] your skin has too much melanin;
[unless] your gender is too fluid;
[unless] you're attracted to the wrong sex.

Then safe spaces turn [dangerous]
our bodies into [hate] crime scenes

in west by god, where gods and monsters
look the same, wild
[not] wonderful and [lily] white.

They say all kinds are welcome here
as six-year-old blood runs
from my head, that rock
that taught me not to be [Black]
on a West Virginia playground.

They say all kinds are welcome here
that there is no place like home
yet these [country] roads to prosperity
are full of [shit] potholes and bigotry

and I'm reminded
at every [impassible] turn
that I don't belong.

Lucien Darjeun Meadows

Where Are You From?

So I am asked, though not as often as many, in grocery store lines, concert ticket lines, climbing into a rideshare, on the first (or thirtieth) day of work. Here in northern Colorado, back east, across the two thousand miles between, and beyond. By an editor, by a publisher, by my partner even though we have known and loved each other for eighteen years and counting. By myself.

There is something about my looks and manner that seems to say I am not "from here," wherever "here" is. (If I were less feminine, less gay, would you still question me so frequently?)

"Where are you from?" Sometimes, "Back east," I reply, or if braver, "Appalachia." But often, if it feels safer, if I might lose just your passing smile (not your permission to rent this home, gain this job, keep walking down this street), I'll reply: "West Virginia."

The truest home I have ever known. The best answer I know. And yet, not entirely true, perhaps.

I was born in Virginia. I have the birth certificate, the photo of the little house, and the pictures of my tiny self, black haired and crying in my mother's, father's, grandmother's arms. We did not live in Virginia long. Depending on who and when I ask, within a few months, or a year, or two, we left for Maryland, a few homes in quick succession, before landing—returning, really, given where many of my parents' parents, and their parents, and theirs and theirs for generations were raised—to West Virginia.

Here, in West Virginia, my earliest memories. Here, the first home I knew, and who knew me. Here, a body blooming amid the crickets and frogs raised in buckets, cardinals and crows in the poplars. The spring flush and the winter silence of the holler who was—is—my sentient, animate world and all my neighbors and friends. Jeweled ladybugs dropped into our well, one by one.

*

"Where are you from?" my partner is asked sometimes, and I envy him his simple, direct answer: "Baltimore." The city he was born in, the city he lived in for almost his first three decades of life. The answer is always the same to "Where are you from?" and "Where did your parents meet?" and "Where were you born?" and "Where were you raised?" and "Where did you first drive a car, first go on a date, first get a job, first get a brother or sister," and on and on. Up this street, the elementary school. Over in that neighborhood, the teenage hangouts. Here, the paper route. Here, here, here—all right here. All Baltimore.

My story is much more muddled.

Say "home" and I see the blue house in the holler. I see the holler folding me back into so much green. The long driveway I'd run up and down, up and down, on the day my father was due to come home from weeks away at work, waiting for the low chug of his truck down the dirt road, the piece of coal shined up in his pocket just for me.

Say "home" and I see West Virginia, I see Monongalia County, I see our house, the dirt road and the holler, the farm across the road where we'd gather for the annual potluck, the ride over to the next town for our mail and Sunday service, the ride over to the next for the one-room library.

Say "home" and I remember the two men who lived together two houses over, always ready with a smile when out in the field, always warm and friendly, but "a couple queer birds," my parents said, never letting me go visit. Whose fields I would find myself near, often, never quite sure why, just watching one or the other working with the land as I stood hidden at the woods' edge.

Say "home" and let me see all of this again, let me bring you back home, down home with me.

But I am looking over my shoulder, I am shuffling my notes, my photographs, knowing that if you keep asking, give me all those questions my partner gets—and his consistent answer, "Baltimore, Baltimore, Baltimore"—I cannot always say "West Virginia," so where does that leave me? Where am I from? Where am I from—that you'll agree, "Yes, you are from there," too?

*

Before high school, my parents moved us back to Maryland, first to a small town house where I remember my little sister, the newest addition to the family, crying and crying. Out our front door, a small patch of trees climbing up a hill—and I would run the twenty (fifty? ten?) feet up the hill, turn around, jump back down the way I came, rolling down in dirt and bruised knees. Again, again, as my sister screamed inside like a rabbit in a trap, my father rocking her fruitlessly.

Not long after, we moved again, to land kept in one branch of my family for five generations. Land who, after my grandparents passed, would be kept for a short while by one strand of relatives before they sold the furniture and linens, then the oven and the pellet stove before foreclosure. Public auction. Scattering, afterward.

Maryland was always described as a temporary move. "We will move back," my father said. "We're going back to West Virginia soon as things get sorted out." I remember him spending evenings on the phone, printing house listings off our first computer, offering them to my mother. Here, "We'd be three miles from a good school." Here, "We'd be right off a paved road." Here, "We'd be close to family." I remember him taking jobs down south, "to check things out," coming back bright with ideas.

We never moved back. He, after several years, moved out. And I, several more years after, moved out also.

A decade since I lived in West Virginia. Over two decades, now. And "Where are you from?" you ask. And I keep saying, "West Virginia, West Virginia."

*

I could try to romanticize my years in West Virginia. I had two parents who still seemed to love each other. I lived with a holler who watched me for hours, for I knew when to find those flowers, these mushrooms, this creek rising, this ridge where you could catch a honey-sweet smell, the direction to look in winter to see the clear-cut edge.

Much of my earlier years are scattered, if not lost, surfacing in sharp moments and vague blurs. If I want to romanticize, I have to blur and silence myself, my family, the land who knew us as we knew them. Haven't many of us blurred and silenced each other enough, already?

The first gay boy I knew committed suicide before he turned eighteen. The second left home and moved north to Baltimore or Philadelphia or New York City, as soon as he graduated from high school. The third lost enough weight that he disappeared for a year, returning always wrapped in a coat, his eyes too large for his face, before disappearing again to live with a man in coastal North Carolina. I don't know if he is still alive. I look for him online sometimes, find nothing—but I don't look too hard, too long, just in case.

I search my university library catalog and databases for echoes of home. Across the Carnegie R1 research library's network, there are zero results for a search of "West Virginia" + home + belonging + queer. I delete "queer," and twenty-three results appear.

*

What does "from" even mean? What does "home" mean? How much "from here" do you need to really, truly, be "from here"?

In his 2012 Appalachian Studies Association keynote address, Si Khan wondered, "How much of being a 'real Appalachian' do we attribute to place of birth, parentage, grandparentage, class, sexual orientation, occupation, ethnicity, language, physical ability, religion, race, culture, education. Do you have to be born Appalachian? Can you decide to become Appalachian? Can you decide you no longer want to be Appalachian?"

"Can you answer the question, 'Where are you from?' in a wrong way?" I ask my partner. "Can you answer it in a way that someone else could say, 'No, you're not,' and you have to agree?"

Place of birth? Virginia. *Place of my parents' births?* Maryland. *Place of their parents' births?* West Virginia, Pennsylvania, Kentucky, Maryland. Each generation before, more West Virginia.

One strand of my family lived since the 1700s in the same (once Virginian, then West Virginian) county for generations, another strand since then also in a neighboring county, and another, and another. My beloved ancestors, without whom I would not be. And yet. There were families already here, for tens of thousands of years. By declaring these mountains their new "home," by declaring their right to remain, my Euro-American ancestors attempted to exterminate the Indigenous peoples who had already been here, *home*, since time immemorial. "Home" as a weapon. Declaring "home" becomes attempted genocide.

No wonder "home" splinters, glass in my hand.

*

Sometimes, my body hurts with the desire to return to the holler, to the deep dark edges furred by trees. Traveling back east for the first time in years, not back home but to Vermont for a writing conference, I come outside each day just before sunrise. I run with soft green paths, lose my breath at breaking out onto a hillside covered and covering me in fog, slowly lifting up the hills.

These Green Mountains are not home. The angle of light is all wrong. I do not know these flowers, this particular cadence of mud and moss. Beyond campus, when I run to the neighboring town, the accent and class and culture are nothing like West Virginia. But if I close my eyes as I slip down these narrow paths, my legs stroked by fern and grass slick with dew, I know I am not in Colorado, and that is almost enough for me to believe I am not too far from home.

*

Where are you from? Where are you from? Where are you from?

One of my great-great-grandmothers blurs. She might be Alheit, Adelie, Barbara—all or some or none of the above. She might have died in this country, or traveled back—where? Close to her in this strand of ancestors is my great-great-grandfather Michael, who died thirty years before my father was born. "Where are you from?" He struggled with this question too, across the distance of years and shifting geopolitical borders. In the 1900 Census, he declared his birthplace, and the birthplace of both of his parents, was Germany. In the 1910 Census, he and his parents were born in Austria. In 1920, Hungary. In 1930, Yugoslavia.

When discussing community and belonging in her 2008 article "'Where' your people from, girl?" Rosalyn Diprose writes that settler-invaded nations create national identity amid a "haunting by a disavowed colonial past." Here, "belonging to homeland (rather than identity) is what is most fundamentally contested," and as a result, questions like "Where are your people from?" are "politically and emotionally loaded." Little wonder, then, that in the 1990 and 2000 US Census, "American" was the most-claimed ancestry for West Virginia.

The miners who marched in Southern West Virginia's Battle of Blair Mountain in 1921 were, as the organizers of the Battle's centennial observance in 2021 wrote, "Blacks who migrated from the South, European immigrants, and white mountaineers." As if the white miners had never been "from" somewhere else. As if these "white mountaineers" are the original peoples of these lands.

No. Like Marilou Awiakta in her 1989 keynote address to the Appalachian Studies Association, I too recognize: "By 'Appalachians' I mean the three major ethnic groups: Native Americans, African Americans and European Americans." Recognize: only one group is *Native*.

Say "Shawnee, Cherokee, Lenape, and Haudenosaunee: the Seneca, Cayuga, Onondaga, Oneida, Mohawk, and Tuscarora." Hold silence for the nations, tribes, bands, and peoples whose names are now lost. Step back and hold space for the nations, tribes, bands, and peoples who are still here—who have always already been here.

*

"Where are you from?" can assume that, wherever you might be from, you are not from "here." You do not belong, fully and unquestionably, "here."

I go walking in a store or on a trail with a darker-skinned Cherokee friend, and someone (usually white) asks her, "Where are you from?" She replies, "North Carolina." But then they say, "No, where are you really from?" Sometimes, she will respond, "I was born and raised in North Carolina." Sometimes, they will push, "But where are your parents from?" (The answer: also, for generations upon generations upon generations, land now sometimes called North Carolina.) They might push again.

We might point the question at them: "Where are you from? Where are your parents from? Where was your family from a hundred years ago? Three hundred? Eight hundred? Where?"

*

One late summer evening, the crickets loud in the stream out front, I ask my partner, "Do you think the answer to 'Where are you from?' could change for someone after they turn eighteen? Could you be 'from' somewhere as a child, and then, after living somewhere else as an adult, become 'from' another place? Can your 'from' change?"

We think for a few minutes, the cool breeze from the foothills breathing through our home.

"I was born and raised in Baltimore," he says. "When I meet someone and they ask, I say that I'm from Baltimore. But, when I'm somewhere else—at a conference, on a vacation—I often say I'm from Fort Collins. Colorado feels more like home than anywhere else I've ever lived."

"Where are you from?" If "you" is this single body, perhaps this answer is the answer to, "Where were you born?" Or, "Where were you raised?" Or, "Where did you spend the most days between birth and age eighteen?"

If "you," though, is the "you" of your family, of which you are just one moment, perhaps this answer is the answer to, "Where were your parents born?" Or, "Where were your grandparents born?" Or, "Where were most of your ancestors in the last several generations born?"

Or, perhaps, simply: "Where have you lived that has most felt like home?"

*

I was born in Virginia. My family is largely from West Virginia and the Appalachian Mountains of North Carolina and Virginia, for about three hundred years. Before then, my Euro-American ancestors came mostly from England and Germany. Perhaps, then, I am also from North Carolina and Virginia, or also from England and Germany, but I have no personal memories of "home" there.

But I cannot easily separate "Where are you from?" and "Where are your folks from?", or, as Audrey Petty titles her 2022 article, "Where your people from." If my direct ancestors had not lived in West Virginia more than any other state for the last few hundred years, I would not be so quick to claim (when I must claim just one state), "I am from West Virginia."

My "from," though, is not the same "from" as someone who was born, raised, and still lives in the same holler, county, state. I cannot claim such close kin. I might be "from," to some extent, but I am not "still here."

*

And I can never "go home," not really, not completely, ever again.

To live openly in West Virginia as queer, as a gay man in a long-term relationship, frightens me. Returning to West Virginia—even claiming identity as "from West Virginia"—can be, as Barbara Ellen Smith and Stephen L. Fisher describe in *Transforming Places: Lessons from Appalachia* (2012), "an act of resistance, a way of fighting back against Appalachian stereotypes." Often, it is enough to love from across a distance.

Sometimes, though, I want nothing more than to roam the woods and hills and rivers of the hollers, but I would be afraid—to smile at my partner, to hold his hand, to catch a quick kiss or hug outdoors, to say "my partner" or more daringly, "he." *Those queer birds.*

Even as the land might invite me back, the humans might not be so welcoming. Home might not—could not—be offered as "home" anymore, to me.

*

"Where are you from?" Where, in other words, have I felt the most at home—even as I know, now, I might feel the least at home there?

A recent June, a Pride Month, and in a big-box store here in Fort Collins, I see socks in the girls' section that stop me, my partner and our cart almost crashing into me: knee-high rainbow socks with "QUEER" in vertical capital letters that march down from just below the knee to just above the ankle. I flush; I turn cold. I want to celebrate that such socks even exist—and in the children's section too!—even as I want to take them all off the rack and hide them behind the light bulbs or dog food. What would it mean to be a teen and to be comfortable wearing such socks? To be a teen and to have your parents allow (or even purchase for you) such socks? To have your friends and teachers smile at you, with you, for you in wearing such socks?

I cannot stretch my mind so far. These socks seem an invitation to violence. We are, after all, just fifty miles from Laramie, Wyoming, and we are in Fort Collins, the same town as the hospital where Matthew Shepard was brought and died. We are in the town that just severed connection with its only local queer youth group after a few parent complaints. We are in the town where I, running the trails as my queer self, have been laughed at, called the typical slurs. And we are in the town of these queer socks.

*

On the phone, my sister says, "Mom and I are looking at houses in West Virginia and thinking of moving back." Surprised, I say my mother refused to move back, say my sister never seemed interested in West Virginia. She says, "We both have a sentimental connection to the state. And we've been going there this summer to march in protests for reproductive rights."

And I sit here, snug in my liberal northern Colorado college town. I am so far from the holler.

I am trying to get back, from writing poems and essays honoring the land who raised me to teaching seminars on working-class writers, where my students read Marilou Awiakta, Diane Gilliam Fisher, and Diane Thiel. But I am two thousand miles away, surrounded by mountains who naturally lose trees toward their heads, where we often go weeks without rain and just four months without snow.

Across the lands within fifteen miles of me, there are three stretches of trail where deciduous trees reach over the trail on both sides, forming a bright tunnel of green, and I know all three. I ache for the summer when I can fold into them, stop on the trail, close my eyes, imagine I am somewhere like home again.

*

I imagine another Lucien who never left West Virginia. Or another Lucien who, when his partner asked, "Where shall we go after graduate school?" rather than saying, "Not back east," said instead, "Back to the rolling blue hills." Who teaches now in one of the colleges, or works as a naturalist in one of the parks, or serves at one of the growing number of nonprofits dedicated to diversity, equity, and inclusion.

Who is "from here," and who "is here"?

Even in New York or Amsterdam, I worry about standing too close to my partner. I worry here in Colorado, when we walk together at dusk and hold hands, and a car comes by. There is no place without fear. Just different shades and degrees. No wonder, when writing as, about, and with queer Appalachians, Anna Rachel Terman, in "Hillbilly Women, Affrilachians, and Queer Mountaineers" (2014), describes existing in a space of "multiple perspectives and debate." Jeff Mann and Julia Watts, in *LGBTQ Fiction and Poetry from Appalachia* (2019), also see a "juxtaposition of identities difficult, confusing, and conflicted." And Hillery Glasby, Sherrie Gradin, and Rachael Ryerson, in *Storytelling in Queer Appalachia* (2020), remind us that Appalachia and queerness are both "multifaceted and impossible to understand as monolithic or singular."

And no doubt, the West Virginia I left was less tolerant and inclusive than the West Virginia who might—who just might—welcome me back home today. The public officials who are passing legislation against reproductive rights, Indigenous rights, anyone-but-straight-white-men's rights are not West Virginia. They are just another irruption of colonialism. This land, these rivers and hollers, have existed for millennia before they were given the name, by some, "West Virginia." And I believe—I have to believe—they will continue for millennia after.

*

In one of the last letters I have from my grandmother, the woman who took me in once I turned eighteen—and who accepted me without questions or hesitations when I at last came out—she ends her letter by writing, "Just always remember where you're from and that you are loved."

"Where are you from?"

From aspen and ash, basswood and beech, wide hands and the forest floor. From Hassel and Harvey and hemlock and hickory—mockernut, pignut, shagbark all. From red maple, red oak, red pine. From pining. From quick glances, borrowed mascara. From Pauline and Pearl. From spruce and sweet gum.

"Where are you from?"

From bee balm, bluebells, and trillium. From rhododendron, redroot, bloodroot, and the red-orange bells of the trumpet creeper. From this land. From mountain laurel, mallow, buttonbush. From the small blooms of the mistflower to the stalks of the scaly blazing star. From watching others disappear and from choosing another route. From ramps, yes, but also the lady's slipper. From here. From right here, love, with you.

Joy Cedar

School Eraser

Erasure *burns*
Slow or fast,
The drag of forgetting
Is never soft

It's an intentional, awful, warm friction
Whispering, "You're gone. You're gone. I made it so you were never here."

It's a quiet, violent thing
To erase people, cultures, histories
It *burns* furious empty holes

Like the ones in the bleached paper
From elementary school
That I pushed the tip of my pencil too hard into sometimes
I tore the paper, but I made it **bold**, did they see? Did they understand?
Could they see me?

Young one, you deserve to know
Who came before

You deserve
To see yourself in their stories
To be curious when you cannot

You deserve intricacy
The past, the pains, the sweetness of the pawpaws

You deserve to learn
To churn
And reconcile

You deserve to be seen, beloved, and you deserve to see

hermelinda cortés

Volver, Volver

Act 1 | Las Posadas

Sometimes on the way home the light hits just right, and I remember as I look over the hills that I believe in some god and that this land feels like some sort of vessel of its body. I smell the creek beds and an early hint of honeysuckle, the musk of damp soil mixed with the cutting of hay. I remember to breathe. Inhale. Exhale. Inhale. Exhale. The sadness expelled from my lungs is overwhelmed by the miraculous. I hold on for dear life, feeling a stirring somewhere—somehow knowing that the ground beneath my feet will catch me no matter how many times I fall, no matter how isolated and abandoned my mind tricks me into thinking I am. That's worth something. That's worth everything really.

There used to be a scuba shop on Route 11, some odd 100 miles from our tin can of a trailer. The closest ocean for scuba diving was four hours away. The ocean might as well have been a whole universe away. Before the scuba shop, or maybe it was after, the building held a small tienda with a collection of piñatas, Mexican dulces, limones, and aguacates. Once a month our familia would make the drive to gather what we couldn't find in any grocery store near us. Most times we traversed on Sundays after mass for the usual staples. Waves of chiles, cumin, and oregano would hit us, seep into our skin, and make us feel alive, connected, and hungry.

On special occasions the piñatas would make the journey home with us. One year, we got a small strawberry-shaped one for my sister's birthday. On the drive back, it nestled like an egg between the three of us in the back seat of our brown Ford Aerostar van. We sat the same way we sat twice a year for the drive from western Virginia to Florencia, Zacatecas, Mexico: the middle seat removed, smelling like clammy children, one of us always needing to inconveniently use the bathroom. One of us singing. One of us sleeping. One of us staring out the window. When we got home, we'd unwrap the crinkly plastic around the red, white, and green coco candies painted the colors of the Mexican flag. We'd blast tapes of ABBA and Tina Turner and Vicente Fernandez and Los Tigres del Norte, content to be at home with our treats.

One summer, a July, with distinct Virginia mountain humidity and coolness of the nights, we watched that strawberry spin for hours, dozens of family members around us, newly minted from border crossing. With our primos, we were overjoyed to beat it with a broomstick, screaming delight hours later after it finally burst under the black locust tree. We took such pride in the piñatas, in cheering on each other, in the sleek braids that held back our dark hair. There was a comfort and a safety in our gatherings. An exuberance for festivity despite the hardships that were in our lives at times. Our backdrop was four trailers settled in the hillsides, next to dairy farms and poultry houses and apple orchards—places of both sustenance and death. The summer was a respite for us. The season brought with it sweet mint tea, garden bounty of tomatillos, jalapeños, pepinos, and squash, and trips to the river. We reveled in the bubble of being with other children of migrants, running the fields, picking mulberries, late night summer parties filled with tamales and arroz and tacos.

In the fall, it was time for school. August brought the county fair and our once-a-year purchase of school shoes. Our bubbles punctured by reality as we returned to the torture of students and teachers who couldn't pronounce our names, who wouldn't let us go to the bathroom, who pinched our ears at water fountains, who thought we were dumber and less capable than our white classmates. There is something that does to a child. The first flush of shame. There was little comfort in the safety of numbers because there were so few of us.

Every day at lunch I sat with two kids named Marcos and Peneth. Marcos was an American-born country Mexicano like me. Peneth was Vietnamese. We were all we had in those hallways and on the playground—fending for each other where we could and providing respite for one another when we couldn't. At lunch, Peneth, shy, honey skinned and rail thin, would mix ketchup and mustard into his mashed potatoes every Wednesday when they were served. I never asked him why and I didn't care. Marcos was near a foot taller than both of us—a gentle giant plagued with all the expectations that came with the size of his body and the color of his skin. At recess, we would turn the kickball into a soccer ball, set up makeshift goals, and pretend we were the world's greatest soccer player, Ronaldo. No one ever left their games of softball and baseball to join us—only yelled profanities that small children yell at other children who look and act different from them. Eventually Marcos and Peneth moved away. By the fifth grade, I tried to make friends with a group of girls bearing witness to all the social signals that I was not to fraternize with boys. I begrudgingly hosted sleepovers at our trailer only to discover that none of them had ever seen a trailer before, that I didn't care to swoon over elementary boyfriends, or care about eye shadow and that somehow all of those things made me an outsider, an other.

We were a family of others.

Act II | La Flor de Zacatecas

Dios te salve María. Llena eres de Gracia. El Señor es contigo. Bendita eres entre todas las mujeres, y bendito el fruto de tu vientre Jesús. Santa María, Madre De Dios, ruega por nosotros, pecadores, ahora y en la hora de nuestra muerte.

"Santa María, Santa María"—we soared through the air. Madre Guadalupe appeared before me. I quit the Catholic Church that year, but my relationship with her was sealed forever in that moment hovering somewhere in a cloud of fog near the Mississippi River in the middle of the night. We were all asleep, including my tío who was driving us three days and three nights from the Blue Ridge Mountains to the Canyon of Tlaltenango. My mom and my sisters weren't with us this time. As an adult, I can't remember why this was the case. I plunge into my memories for answers, but I can find nothing but the resounding feeling of longing and the weightlessness of our car soaring through the air.

A day later, we crossed the border. Several small children climbed onto the bumper of our van. My memory fails me here too. I can't remember being overjoyed or afraid or if they were screaming or laughing. I remember that they did not have shoes.

We drove a day more through the desolate desert of Mexico stopping only for huevos and gas at a roadside stand.

Eventually, the big stone archway of Florencia de Benito Juárez, looming like one of the seven wonders of the world, welcomed us, ushered us through the gateway home. From that portal we made our way to mis abuelos welcomed by the smell of adobe, frijoles, and queso tucked away in rafters. At night we'd pour into the streets of the zócalo. I'd watch the couples swing by arm in arm, young and old, men and women but no other variation to be seen. I was both proud and resentful to be escorted by a male family member on the square. I'd close my eyes and let the sounds and smells of the streets wash me away.

In the mornings we walked the fields, sought the honey out of dead trees on the mountainside, watched the cattle herd around the diminishing lake that could no longer irrigate the maize. We sat in chairs on hillsides eating tortillas and laughing. In the afternoons I would walk to the corner store for chiclets and a Coke and a playdate with mi compañera Perla.

We repeated this ritual year after year, returning to the homeland, nourishing our spirits, collecting pieces of ourselves until we could meet again in the salvation of our ancestors.

But then the cartels came.

Act III | Feast of the Transfiguration

Billy Ray Cyrus was the reason I knew about lesbians. I remembered this forty miles outside of Junction, Texas, just past midnight at a crossroads where a gray fox crossed my path one hot night in July as I drove from Houston to Terlingua. Truth be told, I drove all the way across that giant state just to not think of home, but she followed me anyway.

All the signs were there. The sweating over my best friend, experiments with hair, the discovery of punk music and a CrimethInc. poster wheat pasted on a telephone pole, a great disdain for all things lace. When I finally came out to myself I knew I had to leave the place that had raised me—a survival instinct so many of us follow without a second thought. I quit everything I knew, scattered inside myself, lost to salty tears on country drives in a van we called the pickle. "Leave or die," a refrain whispered by my subconscious and all the ancestors at my back who also knew and lived this truth. When the refrain got loud enough I left for fear of the comfort of death.

I thought I was on my way to Eugene, Oregon, but arrived instead in the old capital of the confederacy, Richmond, Virginia. Where I landed both mattered and didn't. It smelled and tasted different, like trains and dirty river water soaked in heavy air and humidity and the legacy of slave trade. The city petrified me, but its streets also received me, making space to build a version of myself outside of the confines of bloodlines and mountains. The flatness felt like an easier place to see a future—nothing blocking my horizon.

I had only dollars to my name and barely a place to call a bed, but I didn't care. I could wear what I wanted, cut my hair how I liked, fraternize with whoever I fancied and no one cared. I got odd jobs catering and cleaning houses and working in coffee shops. I did Food Not Bombs and found all the other queerdos who had left home on a hope and a prayer to make music and art, to fight the man, to just *be*.

And finally, I discovered organizing, or rather organizing found me, sweeping me into the arms of social movements for justice and liberation, sweeping me into the arms of queer elders.

I accepted it like a baptism, washing over me, transfiguring me, welcoming me to myself. I drove thousands of miles across the South, was initiated into the gift of the lineage of Southern organizing, of queer righteousness to compel ourselves to claim our rightful place in time and place and space.

For years our elders sat around fires telling those of us in our twenties and thirties about the dignity, hope, and courage it took to survive as queer people and we passed along those stories to each other because they are part of our lineage, of how we have loved and how we have made our way in this world that hasn't always and sometimes still doesn't accept us.

In these stories they told us of marches and race riots and the bombings of underground lesbian bars. They grieved in their stories of nursing their gay brothers and comrades to their deaths during the AIDS crises. Their stories included the nightmarish and fear, but they also included the miraculous and the joyous. They told us of poetry readings and karaoke. They told us of lesbian anthologies and gay farms tucked away securely in the country. They told us about the smells of their lovers they would never forget and to never forget the sanctity of convening with chosen family for meals and dancing. They reminded us that regardless of anything wrong with the world, queer people would go on loving each other day in and day out as we have for hundreds of years.

Act IV | Volver, Volver
The way I figured it, the rainforest bordering Appalachia, nestled like a pig in a blanket between the mountains, was the safest bet. Of course, this did not account for the possibility of nuclear war just three hours shy and South of the nation's capital, but it was rumored that the limestone caves could survive it and so I returned and I stayed.

The promise of desire. The whisper returns, "leave or die," and so I leave again, this time for home.

The summer I returned I worked in strawberry fields for a Mennonite. He had four children gallivanting around the fields while I picked slugs off berries. My parents received me in a room I used to share with a sister, converted to a sitting room, back to some semblance of refuge, so I could find myself yet again.

I fell in love almost instantly, wooing a girl with flowers at her art exhibit of vaginas (a typical lesbian affair). That summer felt like possibility. Like I could be home and love a woman. But small town and rural isolation still crept in. The sinking feeling of watching eyes, seeping into and poisoning the air with their cynicism and fear. A stolen bike and a breakup later the surging honeymoon feelings of homecoming subsided into the earth and the sounds of Chavela Vargas.

I drowned myself in local organizing, in booze, in sex, looking for something, always looking for something to soothe the internal chaos of not belonging to a place that you can't extrapolate from your soul. I moved through the daily motions, calmed by the familiarity of the seasons and the markers that shaped my childhood. I watched more queers go than come, but I remained steadfast in staying, more tools at my disposal to survive.

Act V | Pecados y Milagros
In this lifetime I have been many things. My truth is somewhere in these hills. I look under rocks and in the sunlight beaming with a holiness, a

cascading curtain of certainty that I strive to understand. The only thing I know to keep doing is to grind down into this here dirt. Grinding into the shadow side and light side of these mountains replicating rituals from both this lifetime and those tucked away in the hills of Aztlán. This is a place that was chosen and so I stay here, choosing to live in the sacrament of lineage, holy water washing over us when we pause to hear its sound.

I take a detour, drive to the bottom of the mountain to watch the sun fall, looking for something unnamed, unspoken. Trapped by the sight of hemlocks and goldenrod, I feel the air change. A fine mist falls. I follow Hopkins Gap all the way to Fulks Run, watch the summer does prance across the road. I wonder who Hopkins was but know some Fulks by distant relation. At the crossroads there is an old grocery. Here they still have an old soda machine outside and sell Turner Hams. The sign alone gives you the taste of the county fair rolled over in the mouth—instantaneous, dehydrating, salty, a one-of-a-kind pleasure. I inhale the memory, turn over the scent of the hollers, crave a Coke in a glass bottle, ignore the signs for fallen rocks and the promises of the GOP and keep driving. I pass the sign for Bennie's Beach Campground and the first announcements of fall's finest prize—fresh apples. I turn right onto Turleytown through the fog and past the heirs of the Confederacy guarding their front porches like the white knights of yore protecting the finest castles. They don't know they will never get the gold they were promised. Here past the quarry, there is the old white-barked Sycamore that takes my breath away with her breadth and resolute spirit. She is only five miles from my house but it took me a lifetime to arrive here. I pull over and say a prayer at her feet, an anathema amid the Queen Anne's Lace and Milk Thistle in all their glory. The sun continues her daily ritual of rest and I see myself there amid the land that gave me a name, a face, a presence, a reason, a life. Water falls from my heart, and I am whole but for a moment in this place that was never meant for me and that I love anyway, endlessly.

Rayna Momen

Growing Up Black in Appalachia

was like living inside a bubble
like a snow globe always shaken
limited visibility, abandoned
like some junked car
that never did run well
on a full tank of empty hope.

My story was penned
on back roads, in backwoods
on the back of three- and four-wheelers
in underfunded small schools
a perimeter of blissless ignorance.

My [white] mother's hometown
draped in confederate flags
a reunion, where a distant relative
refused us a seat at the table
because my sister and I were Black.

It was driving into city limits
just to find food and resources
our part of the county
counting on everything elsewhere
to survive.

Growing up Black in Appalachia
meant being asked

by neighborhood children,
What's it like living in the Black world?

only some used different [n] words
that burned like crosses
and branded me less than.

It was having your tires slashed
your first cat poisoned.

Growing up Black in Appalachia
made me want to fight and to flee
left me internalized and empowered
to live a double life
like Affrilachians learn to do

to battle the love/hate
for a state that left you wanting

a region
commissioned to oppress.

Joe Tolbert Jr.

To Repel Ghosts

When I was young, I received information filtered through my parents, through their beliefs and experiences. I was taught that God ordained relationships between a man and a woman. I was taught that the foundation of a family was a husband and his wife and that there were no other ways to define what intimate relationships could be. No one prepared me for the break. That moment when old truths became lies and what I once held true needed to be revised. I have learned silence. Silence for survival. Silence for self-preservation. I learned to swallow my desires, and the longing I felt reminded me that nothing is gained without risk.

It is the day after my twenty-seventh birthday. I walk into my parents' house. They are celebration ready. My sister walks into the room with a candlelit cake, and they sing "Happy Birthday," Stevie Wonder style. I wonder if what I am about to do is the right thing to do. Realizing that freedom is on the other side of fear, I blow out the candles and say, "Can you all sit down? I have something I want to tell you." Realizing the seriousness in my tone, they sit down with concerned looks on their faces. The room that only seconds ago was filled with joy and celebration is now suddenly quiet. They are looking at me, waiting, and I sit there silent for a minute. Trying to find the words I know I need to say. "I like men."

See, my parents are both preachers, and I am nervous how they are going to respond. My dad sits in silence, thinking, searching for understanding? I look at my mother. I don't see the love that would normally wrap its arms around me. There is something else there today, an anger welling up inside her, ready to overflow.

"Bullshit," she yells.

I sit there grasping for words that are sure to fail me. My sister takes my mom to her bedroom, grasping for words that are sure to fail her in her attempts to calm our mother down. I hear my mother scream words about God damning me to hell. She refuses to believe that God, who is the essence of love, will still love me as I am.

I always wonder how the ways in which we are taught to shape God at early ages impact the rest of our lives. The way spiritual traditions become dams, blocking our flow into the abundant life of desires fulfilled.

I thought that once this confession was over, I would be free of the ghosts that haunt me, but the truth is that I still have that pause between the safety of what I have learned to be true and the joy of free-falling into my desires. The truth is that sometimes I still don't allow myself the freedom I know I am capable of. Sometimes I contract, bend, and fold, though my heart yearns for infinite expansion.

The truth is that I loved Jason the best way I knew how.

*

Like in most modern love stories, Jason and I met online and exchanged DMs. Our conversation was easy and flowed from our occupations to what we like to do in our free time. Where our people are from. Feeling some level of comfort with each other, he texted me, "When can we meet?" I got nervous because I did not want him to come to Knoxville, my hometown, because I wasn't out. "I will be out of town for work," I said, attempting to divert a meeting altogether. "Where are you going to be working?" he asked. "Dallas," I replied. I was shocked at his response. "Well, you know I can fly to Dallas and meet you there," he said. Caught between fear and curiosity, I replied, "Sure."

I was doing a training in Dallas, and I got a text explaining that he would land in the early evening. I took an Uber to the gayborhood, and to be honest, I was trying to settle into the idea of being out with a man in a public place where everyone was presumed to be gay. I reassured myself that I would be fine because, after all, this was Dallas, not Knoxville. As he walked up to me, I was blown away by how sexy he looked when he wasn't translated by a computer screen.

He was tall, with smooth brown skin and a bald head accentuated by a thick beard sprinkled with salt and pepper. He reached out and gave me a hug, and I fought hard not to melt in his arms. We gave the waiter our drink orders and talked. I said, "It's nice to finally meet you in person and not only talk to you through some kind of screen." "I know," he said, flashing a smile that made me grin. Our drinks arrived. I looked at my glass, a little mad that they didn't have whiskey cubes, wishing I would have ordered my whiskey neat instead. After we finished our drinks, I told him that it was getting late and that I should probably head back. I asked him, "Do you want to come back to my hotel room?" He looked shocked and said, "Yeah. That sounds good."

We arrived back at the hotel, and once he was back in my room, I didn't want my nervousness to make things awkward, so I tried to play it cool. We got undressed, and in an attempt to calm my nerves, I walked over to him and extended my arms, waiting for his embrace. He wrapped his arms around me. Our bodies found their natural sway. I closed my eyes and let my body relax into this new feeling of calm. Finally feeling comfortable, we got into bed. He was the big spoon to my little. I closed my eyes, took a deep breath, exhaled, into the safety of his arms.

*

Like any other Sunday, the church is crowded. Hands are whipping fans back and forth to cool the sweat dripping from their brows. The church is a cacophony.

Amen!

Hallelujah!

Praise the Lord!

The choir is singing, elevating the spirit higher. There is a man who is frequently called on to sing the congregation happy. Let's call him James. He can sing the house down, and if he isn't leading the choir in song, he will be in the kitchen cooking meals that make your taste buds jump for joy like the women do in church. I am a friendly kid, and I run up to James, hugging him. He plops me on his lap to ask me those questions adults ask small children. "How are you doing today? How's school?" After sharing my answers, I walk away with my mother. She admonishes me not to sit on his lap anymore. I am an inquisitive child, so I ask her, "Why?" She replies, "Because I said so."

As I grow older, I question this moment and wonder what set James apart so my mother would say those things to me.

I now realize it's because he is gay.

*

In the bed with Jason, I tried to shake the feeling that my being was wrong. As he held me, I couldn't help thinking about how preachers use scripture to condemn queer people to hell. "If a man lies with a male as with a woman, they have both committed an abomination." I thought about the preachers who declare that same-gender-loving people are destined for disease and damnation if they don't change from their wicked ways.

As he held me, I recalled attending church, the place that strengthened my spirit against an unjust world, and remembered how I was a silent casualty, my spirit deadened by the wrath of God the preachers said was coming my way. It cast shadows of shame over my desire to be held in his arms, loved.

This shame overshadowed me to the point of feeling unlovable, because if God hated me so, how could I ever be worthy of the love of another? Even then in his arms, I was haunted by the ghosts of my past. Ghosts of things I was taught without my permission that make me second-guess the freedom that I have longed for. The freedom that comes with being seen for who I am. I lay there in his arms, wishing I knew how to repel ghosts.

After months of long-distance communication and infrequent trips to Atlanta, Jason finally came to visit me in Knoxville. It would be a lie to say I wasn't nervous, but to be with him in person again made me lean into the discomfort. While watching TV together one afternoon, he turned to me and asked, "Where are all the Black people?" I looked at him and said, matter-of-factly, "This is Knoxville, not Atlanta." Then I flashed a smile letting him know it was all in jest. He quickly shot back, "Smart-ass." We both laughed. Once the laughter died down, I told him that my friend KC invited us to her birthday party. "You want to go?" I asked. He replied, "Yeah, let's go."

We showed the doorman our IDs and descended the stairs to Mirage, a Middle Eastern–themed hookah bar. I heard my friends before I saw them, an eruption of bass-heavy music and KC's signature laugh. When we turned the corner, we were greeted by an all-too-hype birthday girl. I introduced my love to those he hadn't met. The table was a cacophony of Black Joy, each group settling into their own conversations. As I looked around the table, there were no worries, just the excitement of celebrating a friend we loved. However, I was trying to play it cool, constantly aware that he was finally here with me and my friends in Knoxville. I ordered some hot wings and a whiskey ginger. My mind was flooded with questions. Would they like him? Would someone who doesn't know about me see us?

KC looked at me and said "I like him. He's a vibe."

I looked at her, somewhat relieved, and said, "I know, right?"

I was about to speak, and unexpectedly, the music changed. We turned our heads to a woman stealing all the attention. She glided across the room with sky-blue sheer fabric trailing behind her. As she moved her hips, the silver charms on her belt made percussive sounds to bass-heavy Middle Eastern music. KC yelled, "I thought after ten the music changed to something we could dance to?" We all agreed, wondering what made tonight different. I asked the table, "Isn't Sheri's band playing tonight? We should go there." The table agreed, and we all started waving hands trying to locate our server.

The Pit is what I imagine an old-school juke joint to be. As we walked up, you could hear the band playing and smell the mouthwatering scent of barbecue cooking in the smoker. As we turned the corner, I looked out onto a covered patio with strings of lights hanging from the roof. There was a small bar at the end of a row of high-top tables. Opposite the covered patio, there was an assortment of grills and picnic tables. The band was playing some nineties new jack swing, and couples were dancing, men doing a two-step while taking sips from brown bags with the women extending their hands above their heads, clapping to the beat of Black Joy. Everyone was caught up in the energy of memories only a good nineties jam can induce.

I loved how Jason could just throw himself into the thick of the dance floor with reckless abandon. I stood on the wall watching him enjoy himself. He danced his way to me reaching his hand out to mine. With our hands now clasped, he pulled me toward the dance floor, yelling, "C'mon!"

My body became an opposing force determined to remain there, against the wall, surrounded by the safety of friends. There is a way that the body can tell the truth about a person without words, and my body always seems to betray me. This was Knoxville after all, not Atlanta. Sensing my hesitation, he released my hand and found my friend, who is always ready to twerk somethin'. They danced for several songs, and I thought he had found his dance partner in her, but he was relentless, so as I was doing my famous two-step against the wall, he danced to me, again reaching for my hand. Noticing my hesitancy the first time, he didn't pull me to the dance floor. Instead, he pulled me closer to him. He turned me around so that my back was against his body. He wrapped his arms around me and rocked me gently. He leaned his face close to mine. He whispered in my ear, "Don't worry. I got you." I tried to relax, but my hips were stiff with worry that my body would betray me.

*

At some point in elementary school, I learn that the way my body naturally wants to move is wrong. No, it isn't the swish of my hips; it is the angle of my hands. When I walk, my hands become too delicately parallel to the floor. This flourish of my hands makes my life at Maynard Elementary School hard. Walking through the halls, I am greeted by derogatory comments from classmates under their breath but just loud enough for me to hear.

"Look at the way he walks. He walks like a girl!"

"Only a gay nigga would walk like that."

I cry myself to sleep wondering why they say those things about me, not knowing that it is my hands when I walk. One day while running around the house, my mom stops me and says, "Boys don't walk like that." I don't know what to say to her, because all I am doing is walking. I guess I don't walk how most young men do in the early nineties. You know, that walk that has that bop when the next foot would land? If my hands become too feminine, one of my parents points it out to me, telling me that I need to be mindful of my hands.

After my mother connects the dots from the way I walk to the way my classmates call me gay, she says, "If you can't control your hands, ball them into fists when you walk." In my tiny room with the door shut, I practice walking with my hands in fists, not knowing that the fight against the outside world and how they perceive me will one day turn inward. I pace back and forth, thinking of the popular kids who call me gay and how they move with an effortless cool up and down the hallways. I pace back and forth, angry that I can never achieve the cool they don't seem to have to fight for. I begin believing that my body and the ways in which it wants to move are wrong. I start policing myself and not enjoying my body's capacity to know pleasure. I start to distrust my body. I begin constantly questioning if my hands are balled up into fists or if I am walking too much like a girl.

Even now, I can catch myself sometimes walking with my hands balled up into fists or not quite knowing what to do with them when friends take pictures.

*

To not trust your body is to not trust yourself. Every time I close my eyes, I see those ghosts, and all the people who wouldn't let the little version of me be free. In that moment, on the dance floor with Jason, I wish I could have leaned into the joy of our bodies in rhythm to that nineties R&B slow jam. I wish I could have trusted my body's capacity to know pleasure. In that moment, I wish I had trusted myself to be the me I was becoming. On the way home, I couldn't stop my mind from racing. I was mad. I noticed that I was withholding myself from me and from the love he tried to offer too. In that moment, I wish I could have unballed my fists and stopped fighting the man who was there to love me the best way he knew how.

After his visit, I was lying in bed adjusting to being alone again following his departure to Atlanta. My phone rang, and I was excited to see the name of the one I wished was cuddled up beside me. I said, "Hey!" There was a pause. He responded "Hey," in a way that was heavy with something unsaid. I stayed silent, trying to ready myself for what was to come. Sensing that I was waiting for him to finally say what we both could feel being left unsaid, he said, "You may feel that I'm a little distant, but I need some time to figure some stuff out." We all know what it means when someone you were charting a journey of closeness with suddenly wants space. Trying not to let my thoughts and emotions spiral out of control and get the best of me, I told myself that he hadn't said anything yet. I told myself he might tell me something totally different from where I was trying to keep my mind from going. I reminded myself what always happened when I started to fill in the blanks of what I thought was going to happen or what I thought was going to be said. I tried to strip all of the worry from my voice, so I simply replied, "Okay," and hung up the phone.

On the seventh day after he told me he needed space, his name came across my phone again. Someone told me when I was young that the significance of the number seven is that it signals completion. I tried as best I could to prepare myself for what was coming.

"I feel it's best that I end it," he said.

I took a deep breath. "I figured that was the case when you said you needed space." I hung up the phone.

I was scrolling on Instagram trying to distract myself from the swirl of emotions I was feeling inside. My mindless scrolling stopped when I saw a meme with a quote from Ivan Nuru that said, "To the Black boy in love with another Black boy, be patient with yourself. . . . They don't teach this kind of love." To be honest, I was afraid. The freedom that comes from living authentically was always an option for me to choose, but my fear of the ghosts made me withhold that freedom that I so desperately yearned for.

What do I do with this fear? I am realizing that the fear never really goes away, and even if I don't believe it completely, I must begin to try to see myself worthy of love, worthy of living as the me I know myself to be. Love, like light, illuminates us. There was so much I wanted to say to him. I wanted to tell him that I was healing. I wanted to tell him that even though I wasn't where I wanted to be, I wasn't where I started. I wanted to tell him that I was learning to repel the ghosts of my past, that I was trying to love him the best way I knew how.

I have spent so much time and energy trying to figure out how to belong in the spaces around me that I have rarely thought about what it means to belong to myself, to lovingly accept every aspect of myself as I take new forms on this journey. I have gotten lost many times because these ghosts reappear in my life and make me second-guess my direction. I am determined to get back home to myself, and to unlearn all the things I have learned without my permission that have made me afraid to share myself deeply. This has been a process of unraveling, revealing a little more of me each day, but it has been hard to let myself be seen when I have made a home in hiding. I must move forward despite the fear. I am ready to face the ghosts and move past them, continuing to put one foot in front of the other until I find my way to wholeness, the peace that comes with making a home within myself.

*

It is now as it was in the beginning
I am becoming
I will love myself through the journey
I will live knowing that I am a reflection of God
and (s)he makes no mistakes
I will live learning to put one foot in front
of the other toward freedom
knowing freedom is my birthright

May I know deeply that my life is meant for freedom
And that I have what I need to be free
May I remember that my body is a holy room
May I come home to myself
May I heal and repel ghosts that attempt to keep me bound
May I move forward toward freedom despite fear

It is now as it was in the beginning
I am becoming
I am becoming free

Joy Cedar

Copperhead

I put a pencil through a kid's hand once in elementary school

He called me a dyke, you see

I didn't fully understand the word
But I knew he meant it to hurt me

Appalachian and angry,
I told him if he repeated it one more time, I'd slam my pencil in his hand

He looked me in the eye and chanted it

Like a baby copperhead
I acted in a rage and hot shame I did not understand

When we had recess after, I went up behind the school
Up the hill, behind the swings
Where some Ancestors are buried
I picked up the empty chip bags and Pepsi cans to throw away

And I cried, unsure if my parents would be told
Unsure if what I was afraid of was them hearing
The act of retaliation on my part or
If it was that word he used being assigned to me

But next to the graves, cleaning them off until it was time to go in
I felt held in community
We tended to each other, I suppose

I told myself I belonged here
In the only way I knew how to
In a far majority white school, in a town that was named in Tsalagi
A place of push and pull

I wanted to flee // I wanted to cry in its arms

Rae Garringer

Proximity

1.

I remember the bus windows. Fogged up with the hot breath of too many bodies meeting the cold gray dawn outside. A thin line of lavender light above the easternmost ridge. Switchback curves we knew without seeing. Mountains rising naked toward winter skies that hung heavy and close. Many mornings, dawn would break as we turned off Lobelia Road and drove through the Droop Mountain Battlefield State Park, on the first of three buses I rode all the way to Pocahontas County High School. The mountain laurels were thick and tangled in the woods, and the fog filling the valleys, hovering above every creek flowing down into the Greenbrier River, turned the mountaintops into islands. Sometimes the clouds come down to hold us here.

There was a time when I also remembered the name of the boy who, one morning amid my never-ending two-hour bus ride, said, "We should put all the faggots on an island and drop a bomb on them." He then spit tobacco juice into an empty Dr Pepper bottle. That time has long since passed, but I do remember that he was a soft sweetheart of a boy, chubby and bearded already as a freshman, wearing a camo hat and work boots. I know that some reading this will think it impossible for him to be both deeply sweet and violently hateful. I know, too, that others will understand that contradiction, like change, is a rare constant in this life.

I do remember the name of the boy with black hair and glacier-blue eyes who lived in a trailer on top of a long, narrow ridge a few miles from the farm where I was raised. I remember the whispers traveling up and down the aisle of that bus like a virus: that he'd hit it off at the bar with young skinheads from the National Alliance, a neo-Nazi compound up on the hill above Mill Point, West Virginia, an unincorporated town that our school bus also passed through twice each day. And, after the whispers, I remember the "white power" magazine that was passed up and down the aisle, through the hands of every student on that bus. I remember that each of the "Aryan-race" calendars, CDs, books, and clothing items shipped from our very own zip code. I remember my stomach tightening into a ball of stone.

No one I'd ever met had been up that long gravel driveway to the neo-Nazi compound before. My memory of how it was explained to me was that the sheriff had said, "They'd never try anything around here." And that was that. Seemingly enough comfort for the 98 percent of the county that was white.

I wanted to leave more than I had ever wanted anything.

2.

I did leave. First, for college in western Massachusetts, where I quickly discovered both that I was queer and that I was indeed raised in the South (and that Massachusetts is a very different place than my home). I only knew queer people my age who were from coastal cities or who were booking it to New York or the Bay as soon as we graduated. I remember friends, a couple at the time, both of them trans, describing their upcoming move from Northampton to San Francisco. "We aren't stopping once, not even to pee," one of them laughed. It wasn't explicitly stated, but I picked up on the fact that no sane queer person would move home to a place like West Virginia. Not if they had a choice.

I ended up in Austin, Texas. I thought it was just a stop on my way to New Mexico—a state I'd always wanted to visit. But soon after we arrived in Texas, the car that belonged to my then-partner broke down, and then we broke up (after first getting a cat together, of course), and then I had no car or money to move anywhere else, and so I stayed. I became a regular at a gay country bar where cowboys in bedazzled hats and belts would waltz together, two-step real slow. It was the first place I'd ever seen queerness and countryness in the same room, and it became my church for those years of aching homesickness. My friends from the bar would invite me over for Christmas, pick me up in their car since I only had an old rusty bike, and take me to the gay rodeo. When it rained there, I would freeze and listen to that familiar sound: so common at home, so absent in the oppressively sunny blue skies over Texas.

3.

Three years later, in April 2011, I moved back home and rented my neighbor's small house on land that borders the sheep farm where I was raised. The house was built in the early 1900s by the grandparents of another neighbor, now in her seventies, who was raised on the same farm I was—the farm my stepdad bought in the 1970s as part of the back-to-the-land hippie migration. My neighbor told me stories about growing up there, about her grandfather and the day he died, "The day he layed a corpse." She told me about which tree the Baltimore orioles would roost in; that lightning-struck trunk is still there. Down the road a couple miles, at the house where she raised her own family, her husband would be out in the field plowing with two giant muscled Percheron horses. I could see my stepdad's sheep out the window, hear them calling softly to each other across the pasture. There is nothing more comforting to me than the sights and sounds of a flock of sheep grazing nearby.

I was twenty-six when I moved home from Texas that spring. It was then that I learned that during the late 1990s and early 2000s—the same period when I was in high school—the National Alliance in Mill Point, West Virginia, was one of the best-organized and best-financed white supremacist hate groups in the nation. I learned that William Pierce, founder of the group, had been born in Atlanta and college educated in Texas and Colorado. That he had been active in neo-Nazi networks across the United States, including in Oregon, Connecticut, and Washington, DC, before founding The National Alliance in 1974, and later relocating the organization to West Virginia in 1985. I also learned that Pierce wrote multiple books, including *The Turner Diaries*, which inspired the Oklahoma City Bombing, and *Hunter*, which was dedicated to and inspired by the life of a white supremacist serial killer named Joseph Paul Franklin, who murdered at least twenty-two young people across the United States in the late 1970s and early 1980s. The majority of those he killed were Black. The white folks he killed were in interracial relationships.

Joseph Paul Franklin also took responsibility for the murder of two young white women who had been hitchhiking to the Rainbow Gathering and whose bodies were dumped just off Lobelia Road, not ten miles from my home, in 1980. It was later proven, as the community had whispered all along, that it was a good old local boy who was to blame for their deaths. But I'm interested in what led this white supremacist serial killer with deep ties to a national network of neo-Nazis to claim responsibility for the murder of these young hippie women whose bodies were left in the woods along Lobelia Road: a road I spent hours traveling daily by bus in middle and high school, where many of my friends lived, and on which another infamous murder took place which still haunts me to this day.

4.

I'd heard about that other murder on Lobelia Road growing up too. My eighth-grade teacher loved to try to scare me in the afternoons as I waited for the bus, telling me, "My wife won't let me go up that road." I'd heard about a body wrapped in plastic and dumped in a cave. About another body found hanging in a tree. But it wasn't until moving home in my late twenties that I heard the rumor that these two white men, long dead, had possibly been lovers.

It was speculation. Small-town gossip. A childhood neighbor, who has since died, knew one of the men, Peter Hauer. When I asked if he thought the rumor about their queerness was true, he said, "I was at parties with Peter, when he was real drunk, and . . . I could see how he might have been gay." My stepdad, who also knew Peter said, "I've never heard anything about that," and talked about Peter's girlfriend at the time.

This is not a true crime essay. I'm not going to tell you what did or didn't happen, because the truth is I don't care, and I also don't know. I'm not interested in trying to prove or disprove the theories, even the theory that they might have been gay. I'm interested in what it means for young queer people to grow up in a place and time where any evidence of queerness having existed locally has been erased. Where the only evidence of our historical presence bubbles up through rumors of murders. I'm interested in why this haunts me, eats away at me sometimes, and won't fade into the past like it seems to for so many others. I'm interested in what it means to grow up in proximity to so much violence, but largely, to be protected from it.

Their bodies were found in 1975, a decade before I was born. Peter Hauer, hanging in a maple tree, high up on a ridge over a mile away from his house. Walter Smith was found wrapped in plastic inside a cave just a couple hundred yards from Peter's house. He'd been shot multiple times in the head. Not even out of college yet, he was spending the summer in the county, working at Watoga State Park.

The official final verdict by county officials says it was a murder and then suicide by Peter. Some folks speculated that he was disturbed by his desire for the young man. I try to imagine it: him, disgusted with himself for his inability to resist this handsome man. I imagine it festering and growing within him until he killed the boy. Wrapped his body in plastic and dumped it into the cave he'd loved so well. The caves are what brought Peter to West Virginia in the first place as part of the same back-to-the-land hippie migration that brought my parents to the state too. I imagine him going home and typing out a suicide note and then later hanging himself, high up in a tree, on a wooded hillside. So far out it took them months to find his body. Walter was found in June 1975. Peter was still missing at that time. Neither the FBI nor a self-organized group of cavers could locate him for months. The remains of his body weren't found until late fall by a man and his young son who were out hunting for deer and saw his bones tied up in a tree.

But there is nothing more universally rural than the reality of how stories spread and change, like a never-ending game of telephone. And I heard rumors in the county that some people think someone had them both killed. Say there's no way Peter could have hung himself as high up in the tree as he was, that the rope was too short, the logistics impossible. Whispers that someone typed a fake suicide note to cover up a double homicide.

5.

But what if they had been lovers? And what if they had lived?

Grown old together in that house by the cave with a garden full of mortgage lifter tomatoes and scarlet runner beans. Dahlias and yellow roses and rosemary and lavender. Peonies and lettuce and onions. Snapdragons and cosmos and carrots and arugula. Bloody butcher corn and pie pumpkins and gladiolas. Walter would have made his own organic bug spray and spent hours out there combing each leaf of each plant. A spray here, a spray there. And Peter would've rolled his eyes and muttered about how inefficient it was but then gently placed his palm at the base of Walter's neck.

What if they'd made a little heaven together under the shade of that big oak tree next to the house? Trained walls of vines and shrubs to hide their home from the rare passing car winding by. What if they'd dug up rocks to make a little patio one summer before their backs got too old for that much lifting? Peter already stiff and bossing Walter around, who would roll his eyes in return. I imagine they'd have put chairs and a little café table on it, candles to keep the bugs away and to see by. I picture them sitting there, down next to the creek that grew fat and urgent in springtime floods, gurgled quietly in late summer, and sometimes froze over in a long cold January. The ice thick and strong enough to lay down on, to press your ear against, to hear the water still moving slowly deep underneath that frozen surface—and maybe, if you're lucky, even to see a fish, barely moving, looking up at you from under all that ice. They'd drink wine and eat meals from their garden there. Have friends visit from the city in the summer. They'd dance together to their records turned up as loud as they'd go. Sometimes slow and sexy, sometimes wild and far apart.

I want for them to have grown old together, moving beyond the devouring lust and explosive fights of their youth. Moving into a companionship so stable that watching them together was like watching my neighbor's team of work horses at rest, who move in unison even when they aren't harnessed together by leather and metal, aware of the other's body as if it is their own.

Why couldn't they have this too? Why couldn't they have this in a place like this? In this very place? And what would it have meant to grow up here seeing them together at the small-town festival or winning first prize for their prize tomato at the state fair? What would it have been like to ride the bus home—all those wasted hours of kids snorting pills and talking shit and starting fights—if, near the end of the ride, I had passed by their house, wiped the condensation off the window, and waved to them as we drove by.

Would they have seen my queerness before I did? Or would I have found my own sooner if I'd grown up in a community that could have held them gently? Could I have gone to dinner with them in high school, a break from walking on eggshells in my own home? I imagine their house would have smelled like soup on the stove and the last of the year's roses drying in a blue Ball jar on the table. I wonder if it would have been full of art, colorful and cozy. Or if it would have been sparsely decorated with photos cut out of the *New Yorker* and *SUN Magazine*, and the *Pocahontas Times* too, stuck to the walls with push pins, crooked and with no thought for aesthetic spacing. Could I have spent nights at their house, having dance parties on a Friday evening and helping them hang up garlic to dry in the barn loft on Saturday mornings as I did with other neighbors?

6.

The answer, of course, is no. Straight people didn't let their kids stay the night with gay men in the eighties. Or the nineties. Or the 2000s even. Most probably wouldn't still.

And why am I even dreaming up this life of contentment for two men who I never met? Two men who died before I was born. Two men who might very well have been straight. Why am I fixated on wishing they'd had this experience of growing old together in a house they'd turned into a home on a little flat piece of land between Bruffy's Creek and Lobelia Road in Pocahontas County, West Virginia?

"Don't make it a hate crime when you don't even know if they were gay," my stepdad told me in response to my description of the early and chaotic musings of this essay. He has a point. This fantasy isn't even about Peter and Walter. It's about my own famished longing to rewrite the past, to imagine a reality in which rural queer elders could have thrived in this place.

7.

In the summer of 2005, I was home from college, and I was in love for the first time. It was that all-consuming naive kind. I hadn't yet had my heart broken, so I loved unbridled by fear and let it fill me up with all those heights and depths of emotion. All the joy of welcoming in a newfound queerness.

I had buzzed my hair down short and close to my head. I wore a giant ring in my septum, baggy black cargo shorts, a big T-shirt, and a camo hat. I'd go into the gas station, and folks would call me sir and then ma'am when they heard my voice. They still do that, and I smile at their confusion but never clarify. I was home for the summer doing an internship at the "girls" camp I'd gone to all through high school. I spent hours late at night in the office building, laying on the wooden floor holding the landline phone up to my ear, minutes ticking away on the long-distance card, listening to the stories my then-partner told me. He was in San Francisco for the summer working at a queer and trans organization, going to Pride in the Bay, making out with strangers on the street. I was being told by adults who I had found haven with in high school that I couldn't be open about my queerness with the campers, that I couldn't offer support to the first out queer thirteen-year-old who came to camp that year because "Maybe it was just a phase. How can they really know?" I still know that former thirteen-year-old. He's in his thirties now. It wasn't a phase. He is a sweetheart of a trans man, a great dad, a good friend.

That summer, as part of my internship, the organization held a cakewalk as a fundraiser at the tiny nearby town's annual festival. Someone had mentioned that the new head of the National Alliance had gone into the cafeteria where the community meal was taking place. The year before I left for college, William Pierce had died, and a new tensely fluctuating pair of younger leaders had taken over. The Nazis had never come around town events when I was growing up. Not that I knew of. They kept to themselves up on the hillside for the most part.

I didn't know what he looked like, but I remember standing in the sun in the grass between the main brick school building and the cafeteria. I remember holding the broomstick and laughing. I saw a young white man, tall, thin, fit, walking down the sidewalk with a boringly pretty blond woman at his side. We locked eyes. I saw him look me up and down, my black cargo shorts, my buzzed hair. His expression, open and curious, the beginnings of a smile. And then, at the same instant that I realized who he was, he realized that I was not a young skinhead but instead a young faggot, playing with gender.

It feels ridiculous to tell you about his glare. Knowing now what he was capable of, what they were capable of. Knowing that my whiteness and my middle-class upbringing protect me from physical violence so often. But I had never seen someone's face change so quickly to such a deeply hateful glare. It was almost like his eyes changed from open and questioning to the chambers of a gun that he wanted me to know well was aimed straight at my forehead. That he saw me for what I was, for what I am. I can still feel that look in my body. I know there are many who have never experienced that kind of a look, and many more who know it well and are not protected by whiteness from what often follows that glare.

The next year, his coleader was indicted on federal civil rights charges for organizing and participating in brutal attacks against Latinx and Indigenous men at a bar in Salt Lake City, Utah. And so, in the end, the sheriff was right. "They'd never try anything around *here*."

8.

I didn't want to write this essay. Lord knows we don't need more stories about violence, white supremacy, and toxic masculinity in Appalachia. I've seen, heard, and felt firsthand the disdain that so much of this "United States" holds for places like this. There are many people outside this region who only want to hear this story about this place. This tragedy. This racism. This violence. This homophobia.

I've spent years working in radio, documenting rural queer histories, trying to prove to myself and to others that we have always been here, to remind myself that there are long legacies of radical cross-race organizing in these mountains, that this place is not only what national media thinks it is. But it feels like no amount of defending or reframing is enough to shift national ideas about Appalachia. And talking about this violence, these secrets, this hate feels almost like a betrayal of this place that I love so much. Writing it feels like conceding, like switching teams. But the truth is that my community, just like every community, deserves to be understood with nuance, with complexity, with the knowledge that only many contradictory truths taken together make a whole. Each one of us, each one of our homes, deserves at the very least, this. I refuse to let this place be flattened. Ironed out into some monolithic hell hole that serves its role as scapegoat for the rest of the nation.

And yet. This, too, is a part of the place I call home. And not talking about these horrific truths is a way of protecting them, condoning them, even. The complacency of silence, which I also refuse.

9.

How do you live like this? With this deep rage and deep love for seemingly opposing forces and spaces? With this tangled pile of limbs in multiple worlds? Women of color have written this best. Gloria Anzaldúa. Audre Lorde. bell hooks. Toni Morrison. Jesmyn Ward. Louise Erdrich.

I have tried to leave. But it feels like my bones and these mountains are separate pieces of the same puzzle, even as I know that my love of this place was made possible by the attempted genocide and forced removal of thousands of Indigenous people. Sometimes, when I swim in these stories, I don't know why I love West Virginia more than anything else I've ever loved. After all of this, why do I allow this place to hold onto me when it's never told me or my kind that we are wanted, that we are worthy, that we are loved?

10.

I left again. Not because I wanted to but because the resources I needed at the time didn't exist here. First, for graduate school in North Carolina. Then, several years making community radio in the coalfields of eastern Kentucky. But eventually, I moved back home to West Virginia again. Not to Pocahontas County, but close, a few counties away. A place with strong ties and happy childhood memories. A place like home but with just enough space to breathe, to look back with some distance and perspective.

I now live in the little trailer of my dreams, surrounded by animals, under the wise and steady watch of a mountain I love more every day. I can hear the train whistles coming up from the river's edge. Mostly coal trains, sometimes Amtrak. And most mornings, I can see the fog hugging the river's surface down in the valley. Some days, I'm convinced I will never get laid again. And sometimes I wonder if my obsession with imagining a happy, long, stable love for two men who were probably straight, who died a decade before I was born, is only born of selfishness. Because still, today, I'm uncertain if I can have this kind of life, this kind of love, in this kind of place. After years of gathering rural queer histories across the continent for *Country Queers*, I still feel like I have to invent them for myself in the place I call home. Maybe writing queer history into existence in a place where it was all but eradicated is my attempt at reclaiming my home for my own and our collective queer futures. But most days, I'm okay with that if it means I get to be here. In these mountains. In the only place I've ever truly been able to rest.

In Dorothy Allison's memoir, she writes about how it's possible to both love and hate the things we aren't sure we understand. I don't know how to wrangle this essay into a neatly flowing whole. These layers and tangles of violence across time and space. This undying, aching love for this place. But maybe that's just it: that hate and love aren't actually binaries in opposition to one another. That old familiar lie that keeps trapping us in bodies, patterns, and stories that limit possibility. But instead, they, too, exist on a continuum, a spectrum with millions of points along the way and beyond. And just like gender, just like desire, just like rage, or sadness, or euphoria—we never exist at only one point on that continuum for long. We are constantly changing and shifting. Rarely understanding the things that truly matter in this life, until long after they're gone.

And this tangle of stories, this dense briar bramble I can't find a neat way through—I have to write it. Because I want these community ghosts that haunt us to be released. I want them to be free to finally rest. I want for those of us still living to be able to rest. I want for us to believe that we can create a radically different future here. And I want us to get to work on building it together. Joyfully, lovingly, queerly. I want our communities to heal so that we can hold and see one another with more grace, so that we all can have a little more room to breathe.

Brandon Sun Eagle Jent

Circles/Dances

I. Northern Kentucky, 1998

Momma drives her red Chevy to every powwow in the state
so we can feel the drum's heartbeat pulse in our chests.
Mallets beating stretched rawhide, the high-pitched wail
of powwow singers braiding vocables
into melodies, call and response. Jingling
dresses, rainbow fringe and feathers swirling,
dancers float inside the circle, their prayers rising
on waves of white sage and sweetgrass smoke.
Oily frybread, hands glistening, buffalo chili
blooms maroon on white paper plates.

"Do you want to dance?" Uncle asks me, gesturing to the circle.
Right foot raised, tiptoe tapping, foot flattening, left repeats.
A bashful child, head shaking horizontal, my gaze sets
on the drummers, lost in their lightning strikes
rippling across the hardwood floor like raindrops
on a still pond, reminding all in the circle
we are one mind, one heart, a web
woven into one life.

II. Southeastern Kentucky, 2013

Mamaw dances every Saturday at the local community center
so she can feel those mountain songs in the soles of her feet.
Powdery perfume and warm tobacco smoke rises
in waves from beaded blouses and collared shirts
as she leans in to greet senior citizens. A live bluegrass band

blares over tables of idle chatter, Styrofoam squeaking,
plastic forks plunged in yellow-white mounds
of chicken and dumplings, half runner green beans
anointed with fatback, a baptism of black pepper.

"Do you want to dance?" I ask her, gesturing to the dance floor.
Shuffle right, shuffle right, shuffle left, repeat—
pairs of dancers promenade in little circles all around.
My gaze travels from her shoulder and lands
on the band, fingers striking banjo strings,
the high-pitched wail of bluegrass singers:
Will the circle be unbroken? / By and by, Lord, by and by.
I give Mamaw a twirl and the thunder claps,
rain pounding windowpanes outside like a drum.
We weave two generations into one embrace,
one mind, one heart, in the middle of our circle.

Rayna Momen

Dear West Virginia

The day you stopped fighting
my love for my partner
with the blunt bigotry of your ban
was the first day
of the rest of my life

yet it took you so long to surrender
your white flag barely waving
amid the smog
all those slurs fired
from rusty musket mouths

picket signs and sermons
declarations
that we deserved to burn because
we were born the wrong sex
and just happened to fall in love

our androgyny a fraudulent threat
our bodies unsolved crimes.

And today I forgive you
your topless mountains, hardly
the majesties they once were

your legislature gone wild
your not-so-wonderful whites
your epidemics
your prominent hate

and I'm learning to embrace you
your bluegrass, your moonshine
your poverty and
unparalleled resistance

your statistics
that put us on the map
for reasons I would rather forget.

Jai Arun Ravine

What Anchors You Here

Mash

Mash four overripe bananas with a fork. Use ones with the most black spots. Mix in buckwheat flour, wildflower honey, soy milk, canola oil, and hard clumps of raisins. Pour into a loaf pan and bake. Use your fingers to lick the bowl clean.

You pull back the curtains and fiddle with the blinds. You see the pots of anise hyssop and Thai basil you manage to keep alive, the sprawling pumpkin patch burst from composted seeds, the huge tulip magnolia past its first bloom. You hear the skittering screech of raccoons, the wailing yowls of community cats, a mockingbird cycling through their catalog of calls. You see the grassy lot across the street and the concrete steps up from the sidewalk, and your neighbor on move-in day yelling, "Hey that's not a park, it's my yard!" You see the land as it once was, held in common by the Shawnee and the deer—as it is, with fences and cell phone dramas and whining lawnmowers—and as it will be, turned to dust.

Your mom is Thai, an international student from Thailand. Her parents are photographs. Your dad is white. His parents met in Radford, Virginia. Your dad's dad enlisted in World War II, drove a boat onto the beach at Normandy, went to Virginia Polytechnic Institute on the GI, became a civil engineer, helped design the Blue Ridge Parkway. Your dad's mom was the principal at Fort Hill Elementary, read a lot of Anne McCaffrey, smoked Virginia Slims. Your mom worked as a clerk at JC Penney and a receptionist at Saint Francis Hospital, loved Fashion Television and travel shows and cheap deals and Édith Piaf, clothed you in last year's Gap and Gabe's clearance rack. Your dad worked at Charleston Newspapers, is a nature photographer, loves hiking and science fiction and cool rocks, is responsible for introducing you to Kerouac and Poe. Your parents met at West Virginia State College where your mom was sewing beautiful fabric hangings from Thai silk. No physical evidence of them remains.

You get on your bike and coast downhill. At the bottom, you pass the perpetual antiabortion protesters on the corner across from the Women's Health Center. Somebody x yards away hollers, "Do you have a lighter?" You pass a boarded-up house every other block. You know the only jobs here are food service or Dollar General. You pass the Kroger or the gas station or the detention center and some guy catcalls you. You know the cycles of addiction and poverty and abuse and homelessness keep spinning. You know that instead of prioritizing mental health, the state makes it a crime just to be alive. You know the land and its people have been disenfranchised. You know that Indigenous cosmologies and technologies value reciprocity between humans, animals, plants, water, land. You know that now, land is something to be owned, something to be turned for profit. You drive the twenty or thirty minutes to your partner's parents' place. The more space between houses, the more Trump/Mooney, I Hate Liberals, Friends of Coal bumper stickers. The more green it gets, the more Fuck Biden, Trump 2024, Fuck Your Feelings, "Back the Blue" flags. Imagine. That flag and you, flapping through the same air.

Crumble

Crumble a block of tofu with your hands. Cook it down with onions and Ragu chunky vegetable tomato sauce. In a baking dish, layer the tofu and tomato mixture, lasagna noodles, and thin slices of eggplant and carrot and zucchini. Top with shredded mozzarella. Bake until bubbling and crispy.

You mix and match your partner's old clothes with clearance rack items from Marshalls with your mom's old jewelry because it feels like healing. You leave "sex" blank on intake forms or write in a field for your pronouns or just stop caring. You get nervous every time you see a cop car. You get pulled over for an out taillight at 9:00 p.m. on a Sunday one minute from your house. The cop asks to see your partner's ID, says, "you're going the wrong way if you're coming from there," says, "it'll be easier if you just tell me where the drugs are now," says, "do you mind if I search your car?" says "whatever you are." Because your partner starts stuttering with anxiety. Because you get angry and defensive when he calls you "ma'am." Because it's the end of the month. Because it's the West Side. You don't stop thinking about privilege and race and class and place and power, you go through so many extra steps just to get out of your house, just to prepare for and protect yourself from the onslaught of the world, and all this is absolutely invisible, all this never once crosses the field of perception of the people you pass.

You have a graduate degree and ten years nonprofit admin and communications experience, but your trauma and your social anxiety leave you feeling inadequate and incompetent and unable to sustain a full-time job. You play Cooking Mama and DDR and Pokémon Stadium and Blokus and Connect Four and Bandu. You do crossword puzzles. You go on walks and hikes and walks and hikes. You scritch, comb, and pick ticks off the dogs. You modify old T-shirts and sew weird dolls and string beads together. You cradle and cuddle your bapies (and by bapies, you mean your cat, who interrupts and sits on your paper at the exact moment you write this), and when she starts to lick your hand or your nose and purr so hard she chirps, you don't want to get up even if you have to pee. You go to the antique mall just to look at old stuff, to the T.J. Maxx just to smell the candles. You're always in a Dollar Tree.

If you meet someone who is also queer or trans or nonbinary and/or Asian and lives in West Virginia, you will immediately want to ask them all the questions and spill your life story and be besties and invite them for dinner and be intimate witnesses on each other's spiritual journey. But in fact, they'll probably be strangers. In fact, you'll probably never see them again. In fact, you've probably never met.

"Hi, I'm half" is the sentence that tumbles and wrestles and burrows down in your core.

Simmer

You make curry because somehow it's something you think you know how to do. You know to take chicken or tofu and a can of bamboo shoots and carrots and potatoes and coconut milk and put it over jasmine rice. You make it in an old yellow pressure cooker with no pressure from the thrift store with a package of curry paste your mom gave you: dark red, almost brown, slightly clumpy, neither wet nor dry. In hindsight, knowing your mom, the curry paste may have been past its expiration date. In hindsight, knowing yourself, the curry paste may have crossed one too many states, may have sat alone in the cold humid dark for one month too many. In any case, sharing a kitchen in a house with four other strangers and having to cook a weekly communal meal, you learn that your curry is a concept no one wants to eat.

When you're sixteen or seventeen or eighteen you write a poem called "Asian Appalachian." You know having a Thai mother makes you different. You know your milk, bread, and lunch box don't smell like other kids' milk, bread, and lunch boxes. You know to hide your whiteness, your Thainess, your scarcity, your queerness, your street address, your mother's immigration status, your anger, your depression, your feelings. You know you're two. Mother, father, male, female, East, West, good, evil, right, wrong. Both, and. You know that in your presence, white people feel permitted to launch into long stories about their travels in Thailand without any regard for what the country means to you. You know that the silence and the distance between your parents have come to define you.

For nine months, you price shipments and stock shelves at the International Grocery in Kanawha City, run since 1997 by an Indian American couple in their late sixties. You ask Meena for a job because your mother frequented the store back then for bulk tofu, and twenty-five years later, Meena still remembers your mom for her big, beautiful smile and silver-white hair. Between an ancient price gun, a handwritten inventory, and recycled cardboard and tape display boxes, you see so many kinds of folks: Indian, Pakistani, Bangladeshi, Filipino, Ghanaian, Iranian, Lebanese; white veterans in flannel who drive two hours for big buckets of kimchi; a Romany woman with a husband in a kilt and a long-haired son named Moon; pushy young Nigerian women; smiling chill uncles and bossy aunties; tall awkward teen boys; fly Jamaican sisters; a gay couple with a YouTube cooking channel; intergenerational families; girls who karate kick the rice bags; Black folks with food trucks; distraught and disdainful Chinese grandmas; white couples who want to "experiment", disgruntled doctors; and an adorable Korean grandmother with a country accent. They're all here from other places, getting a PhD in engineering or medicine, running a restaurant or catering business, or following a family member with one, the other, or both. The ones who are married with two or three children already—you know they're younger than you.

You know that being Asian and living in West Virginia is far from an organizing strategy. It's minding your own business, it's driving two hours for groceries you recognize, it's staying under the radar, it's straight As or else, it's feeding and clothing and teaching your kids and your grandkids and great-grandkids with your blood and your tears and your bones.

But still. Every time you see an Asian person on the street, you stare. Even though you know you have nothing in common with them except a metaphorical umbrella, still. Every time you see a mixed-race kid, you stare. And not once do they notice you. Not once do they even meet your gaze. You wonder why they don't seem to need the validation you crave.

You bike past the historical markers on the pedestrian path along the Kanawha (or "Chemical") River. You know that these signs mark the lives and deaths or white settlers, and that the mansions across the boulevard, now offices, once belonged to coal, salt, or timber barons. You know the history of extractive industries and exploitative labor practices that have irreparably scarred this land. You know about the strip mining, the fracking, the pipeline construction, and the resistance to it. You know about the incredible history of union organizing across race. You know about the water, the environmental cancers. You know about the ecotourism, the state parks, the trails, the white-water rafting. You pass abandoned heaps of clothing, Icehouse EDGE empties, emotional love letters scrawled in permanent marker on metal railings. You know that everyone knows someone who's gone. Out of state. Overdosed. On the paved pedestrian path, not painted for bike lanes but used by many a biker nonetheless, some guy has the nerve to tell you, "The road is over there."

Cut

You remember your mother meticulously cutting off every bit of fat from the chicken. You remember how she peeled mangoes. You remember how she made curry, not with an aromatic paste or a turmeric-based spice mix or even coconut milk, but with a red-orange powder from Penzeys and yogurt. You remember how the leftovers congealed in the fridge in plastic containers. You remember how she deftly cut a block of tofu, holding it over the wok with her left hand, her right wielding the knife.

In a coma, off the respirator, alone in the ICU, your mother takes her last breath on the morning of Call to Action for Racial Equality's huge Black Lives Matter rally downtown at the capitol. You only realize this later that evening, when an aunt on your dad's side, not an aunt related by blood but by marriage, as if it matters, with whom you have no relationship other than having shared the same space as a child, says, "Why do they want to take down our statues? Our statues are our history." Because your grief is too new, you simply un-hear it.

You un-hear it a couple of days later when your oldest cousin on your dad's side, related to you by blood, as if it matters, with whom you have no relationship other than having shared the same space as a child, points her phone toward you. When this cousin, a Rite Aid manager, shows you a picture of a woman who happens to be Black, who happens to be stealing shampoo from her store. When this cousin pointedly turns her head left and then right and then says the n-word. When no one around the restaurant table does anything. When your aunt, related to you by blood, and this time, maybe, it matters, makes eye contact and a small laugh, not to sympathize with you but because she knows this is the kind of thing that would make you upset.

When this aunt tells you she was in the room at Cabell County hospital in Huntington when your mother, offered an epidural, asked how much it cost, and then, instead, closed her eyes and bore down, without any painkillers or insurance at all, bringing you bloody into this world. When your aunt makes eggrolls the night your mom dies because it was something your mom taught her how to do, which touches you even though you never remember your mom making eggrolls for you. When your aunt pulls strings and out of nowhere hooks you up with a discounted cremation service. When your aunt says that even though your mom is no longer her sister-in-law, "she's still my sister." When your aunt, hearing about the ACLU and Planned Parenthood event you attended, reminds you she is not pro-choice, and it shouldn't surprise you but it does, because you're related by blood, because you're sharing the same space. When your aunt lets you attempt sleep in her small spare bedroom crammed full of antiques for two weeks. When your aunt tells you a story about her grandparents or your great-grandparents in Bedford or Tazewell County, Virginia, and you don't know how to tell her that repeating a story about someone else saying a racial slur is still a racial slur. When your aunt is paying for your dinner because your mom just died, you simply un-hear it.

Because the grief is too new. Because the Lexapro and the melatonin and the hard cider and the calls and texts and emails from chosen fam, you put on your mom's hat and rings and bracelets. You dance next to your aunt and cousin out by the river at Live on the Levee to a Fleetwood Mac tribute band because your mom loved Stevie Nicks and so do you. Because the grief is too new, you simply un-hear it. It's what your mom would do.

Salvage

Start with a little bit of coconut oil and Chaokoh coconut milk. Add just under half of the little tin of Maesri green curry paste until it starts to bubble. Add your thinly sliced pork until it's mostly cooked. Add your chunks of eggplant and mushroom and the rest of the coconut milk. Simmer covered until the vegetables soften. Add palm sugar and fish sauce. Turn off the heat. Add Thai basil. Let sit. Spoon over rice. It will be even better the next day.

The next day, during the total solar eclipse, you enter your mom's garage apartment in Roane County for the first and last time. For seven or eight years, she was a home health-care aide for an elderly white woman with Alzheimer's. You see the bed where she watched Matt Smith–era Doctor Who marathons and fangirled about them later with you on the phone. You see the lawn darkening as you count her cash and wade through piles of scissors and coins and items foraged from the trash and old plastic containers and piles of really nice clothes that don't fit you and magazines, and you wonder what to salvage, what could feasibly fit into the backseat of a car, what to keep since you are never coming back here.

When you leave, West Virginia follows you. Everyone's first question is always some version of "How?"

When you return, West Virginia follows you. Everyone's first question is always some version of "Why?"

You try telling stories about being the best at hiding in spotlight tag, the hedges becoming tunnels, heavy with snow, going on stupid made-up missions in your yard at night pretending to be La Femme Nikita. You try telling stories about the children's floor of the library or the basement of the Little Theater or the cemetery at the top of the hill. You try telling stories about being buried in your journal or your book or your body. Eventually, you avoid telling a story altogether.

In South Charleston, at the end of D Street and Seventh Avenue is a landmark known as The Mound. Before the Christian Era there were the Adena, the Indigenous peoples of this region colloquially known as "the mound-builders."

You walk around and up along the circumference of The Mound to the top, which was leveled in the 1840s so a horse-race announcer could gain enough vantage to call the shots. You walk up there and stand on the Adena's dead. You think about how the anchor for this little neighborhood is a hill where people are buried. You think about how your mother's death anchors you here.

You walk down and around and one block southwest to the Asian Market, run by an intergenerational Chinese family whose members sit on stools and watch dramas on their phones, ride hoverboards through the aisles and do ESL homework, and have no interest in who you are. You go to the Asian Market because you need coconut milk and tofu and that chrysanthemum drink and probably something else.

You walk back to The Mound and one block southeast to Pho Vinh Long because you need the small no. 16 or the grilled pork bún. You don't mind watching again and again their Vietnam tourism DVD on loop, because you need noodles. You walk across the street to Yen's because you need an avocado or taro smoothie with boba or a Thai iced tea.

You walk back to The Mound and back toward the Asian Market to the new Thai place that opened because you need. You walk into Elephant Thai like you've walked into every Thai restaurant you've ever been to in your entire life, because you need. You sit and watch the DVD of an outdoor classical dance performance or the stream of Thai pop music videos or Mark Wiens in Sukhothai and you order the yum woon sen and the iced green milk tea because you need to prove something. "Hello, my mom is Thai" is the first secret you desperately want to tell.

Imagine your mother journeying through all of time and space with David Tennant in the TARDIS. Imagine she's not dependent on him, she's not in love with him, she's not searching for validation from him. Imagine she has her own agency. She believes in herself. She asks for help and knows it as a sign of strength. She experiences her vulnerability as power. She asks for what she needs to heal. She has impeccable style and fabulous outfits and sassy wit. She laughs. She shakes her mane of silver hair, aglow. She has her hand behind the wheel, on the lever, she turns the knob and opens doors. She drives. She's traveling. She's on an adventure.

This essay is dedicated to my mom (1945–2017). Special thanks to RayRay and @RinSilpachai.

Brandon Sun Eagle Jent

Kentucky Waltz

Our clothes make acquaintances
in puddles on the floor,
ripples of bedsheets cascading
from the mattress. Clouds of sweat and musk
condense, a perfume of pheromones
pulsing through the room. The full moon
penetrates the bare window, slowly
revealing two musicians, rehearsing,
heartbeats like bass lines, percussive
panting. I quiver, his bow glissandos
across my waiting fiddle strings,
he drones in response to fingered
chords upon his banjo.
He takes the lead, pounding out
the rhythm, tempo allegro:
one, two three
one, two three
slow, quick quick
slow, quick quick.
He pauses, relieves pent-up pressure
on his tender tuning peg,
careful not to break a string,
grind the waltz to a halt. We switch
positions, both hungry to swap
ballads, lips parted and greedy,
more, more, faster!
Morning comes in gushes, warm
light dripping down the walls.

The moon aroused once more,
I realized we had sung nothing
but love songs the whole night through.
I never learned his name.
I haven't seen him since.

G. Samantha Rosenthal

A Queer Place Called Home

> At the dawn of the next new moon, there will be something waiting for you at the crossing of the skeleton and the butterfly garden.
> —Mo

I.

I have been dreaming of buying a big house in my neighborhood and inviting queer and trans people to live with me in it. I have had this dream for many years, but now feels like the time to do it. I have never owned property. I've been a renter my entire life. Yet the big queer house feels suddenly within reach—financially, logistically, creatively.

Yesterday, my lover and I spent the afternoon on a rural farm—fifty miles south of Roanoke amid rolling brown hills. Our feet crunched on winter's dried-up grasses. I kept gathering clumps of hay and mud and weeds in my hands and smelling them. The land in January smells amazing. Liza tells us they hope to bring queer people together in this space, to live, to farm, to share community. It sounds like a dream. It sounds possible.

As queer and trans people without the privileges afforded to cis white men, I think that whatever we can do to carve out spaces of safety and belonging, we should try it. While so many queers do buy property yet replicate heteronormative domestic patterns, I know how badly we need spaces that support alternative modes of kinship and community. We still need collective spaces. And I want to live in a house with other queer people.

Queer collectives are not magical places immune from harmful actions and consequences. These are the real messy spaces that queer people always make. But we ought to try to make spaces that support and nurture nonheteronormative lives, that foster creative forms of kinship and community, that provide affordable housing for queer and trans kin.

I have had two experiences with motherhood: one with a genderqueer teenager I met when they were fifteen, the other with my dog. My teenager is now twenty. He's off at college in Richmond. He came from a stable home and has a supportive biological family. Indeed, before my child learned to drive, his bio mom would drive him to the local LGBTQIA2S+ community center to spend time with me and his many-gendered mothers. He attended all of the Jewish holidays in my home for several years. Recently he visited from college and introduced me to his sweetheart.

I took my dog, June, in when she was two months old. My friend from Asheville drove her up to Boone for the handoff. She threw up two times in their car. I drove June home with me to Southwest Virginia. During the ride, she sprawled out in the passenger seat, all twelve pounds stretched out like pizza dough beneath a rolling pin. At one point, I glanced over while driving. She was so still. Her tongue hung slightly outside of the front of her teeth. My immediate thought was that she was dead—she had died in our first hours together because I failed to give her what she needed. I didn't know what that was.

Sometimes I think motherhood is simply this: being needed. That to mother is to be called upon to care. Sometimes I find myself talking out loud to June about how hard I am working for her—"do you realize what it takes to put food on the table and to pay for your veterinarian visits and all these toys and treats?" But then I'll catch her resting in her bed on her back with her legs splayed open, her neck crooked to one side, her tongue out like it was on that first day. I study her. I can see that she is safe, she is comfortable. To lie on her back like that, to be so vulnerable. I can't even do that.

I grew up in a good home. For my first seven years, we lived on a suburban street where the houses had just been built. There are pictures of my older brother and mom and dad standing on the site of our house before construction. This is the suburban dream of newness. We were the first occupants of our first home.

In second grade, we moved a mile away to another corner of the same upstate New York town. Our newest home was also a 1980s-era domicile. The original owners had designed the house to fit their family, including a pink bedroom for a girl and a blue bedroom for a boy. Strangely, my cisgender brother got the pink room, and my own strange boyhood unfolded inside the blue one.

My parents still live in that house. They have lived there for over thirty years. It is a home that contains infinite memories, each person remembering different things about it. Fights that involved family members throwing objects across the room, hiding in the basement behind the hot water heater listening to my parents argue through cracks in the ceiling, secret sex with high school girlfriends in more rooms of the house than not, secret cross-dressing in my mother's clothes, looking at myself in my mother's vanity, trees coming down and going up, rabbits, deer, and foxes and mosquitoes the size of coins.

I guess everything we were doing in that house was family. It is all part of enacting that thing that most people want—this replication of a model passed down to us from our parents, desperately trying not to emulate them. I have had countless conversations with queer friends about family as a locus of trauma. I like to think of our houses not just as ruins. The memories live primarily in our minds, not in the walls. Someday, new people will live in that house, and nothing we did in it will matter to them, just as the pink and blue bedroom children are probably in their forties now. I wonder if they are cis.

Everyone has COVID-19 now. My friend calls it the "queer wave" because it is rippling through our community, through our neighborhood. In isolation my friends bring over soup and soap and honey and cookies and plants and handwritten letters and a coloring book. And then, I am cooking and delivering soups and muffins and plants to them. We make Spotify playlists for one another. My ex grants me her Showtime log-in so I can watch *The L Word: Generation Q*. I guess this is what Hil Malatino means by trans care.

We are living through an age of mass illness and mass death. The state is doing jack shit. They don't care about us. Friends and lovers have started mutual aid organizations. They have distributed tens of thousands of dollars of groceries to those in need. Queer and trans people are doing this.

I don't like the term chosen family. It suggests that the opposite— biological family—is not chosen. But I know that, as adults, we actively choose whether or not we want to be in kinship with our bio kin. Some people say family is for life, but I was surprised to discover that there are no rules and no enforcement of that maxim. We have the freedom to associate with whomever we wish. There are members of my own biological family who have separated from us, and I like to think that they are living well because they made the right choice.

I prefer the term queer family because queer suggests that the idea of family itself is in need of revolution. Queer family is not just about replicating heteronormative kinship structures—cohabitation, child-rearing, nuclear households, marriage—but challenging the basis upon which we consider some groupings of people to be familial and others not. It is about recognizing the state's role in shaping the legality and financial viability of what a family is and reimagining and manifesting alternatives to that model of kinship.

I began to understand queer family when I made transgenerational friendships in Southwest Virginia, when sixty-year-old lesbians and trans women became my mothers, when I adopted a genderqueer teenager as my child. Queer kinship is me putting your name down as my emergency contact and listing you as the beneficiary in my will. Queer kinship is building relationships that transcend age and categorization, bonds that flirt with the messy borders of love and intimacy and belonging, where we show up for one another under all circumstances, where we hold one another and cry in each other's arms when no one else is there to hold us.

My realtor is a twentysomething blond woman with wispy straight hair and a devilish smile. She makes ridiculously cute videos of herself dancing and lip-synching to pop songs and posts these on the same social media page she uses for business. I tell a friend that she and I make a good team because we both bring a wild femme energy to the home-buying process. If I am going to participate in this capitalist shitshow that is the ongoing commodification of the human right to shelter, then it should at least be as campy as hell.

Just one year ago, it was legal for home sellers and lenders and real estate agents and everyone else to discriminate against me in Virginia because I am trans. I got my last apartment in Roanoke by dressing in drag as a boy. If that's not camp, I don't know what is. I had just started hormone therapy, and my whole body flinched whenever I was referred to by my birth name or when my landlord used he/him pronouns. In the apartment prior to that, I used to plan the times I would sneak out in dresses and makeup so that my upstairs neighbor would not see me. One day, the kids from upstairs came running around the exterior of my first-floor unit, banging on my windows, screaming, "Are you gay? Are you gay?" I hit the floor. I crunched my body up, held my breath, as if bullets were flying through the windowpanes and I was saving a life.

II.

As children, our first experiences of belonging are with our family. When we attend grade school or summer camp, we wonder if we belong among peers. When I was in my twenties, as a recent college graduate, I felt desperately unmoored. I hoped to latch onto a life partner. I married one. It didn't work out. At forty, I don't even know what family is anymore. Perhaps I have read too much queer theory.

Yesterday, a lesbian couple in Southwest Virginia messaged a large group chat of rural queers announcing that their sperm donor had backed out. They were looking for someone new, someone queer, to give them sperm. I am a queer person with sperm, but I can't predict what state those sperm are in. In *Detransition, Baby*, we witness the fantastical story of a detransitioned trans woman who also thought her sperm were lifeless—yet, then she makes a baby. In another fantastical twist, Torrey Peters never explains how Katrina may have responded to Ames's breasts after six years of hormone therapy. When I finished the book, I slammed it on the couch: *what about Amy's boobs*?

And what about these breasts—my tits? When the lab work comes in after my second tranniversary—celebrating two years on hormones—the doc says everything looks fine. But I am astounded to read that my estradiol level is over 1,000 pg/ml, and my testosterone level is abysmal. That's what you want to see, he says. It also could be because I swallowed my pills just before drawing blood.

A quick internet search demonstrates that my estradiol level was equal to that of a woman in her first trimester. It's why when people tell me I don't look my age and they ask what my skincare routine is, I say: estrogen. I glow. Indeed, I do think my body is pregnant. But instead of fostering a new life, I'm putting all of that hormonal energy into remaking this butt and these boobs. The blue pills have given me a pregnant body without child.

I go on a date with a trans woman, and she says estradiol levels above one thousand means your bones will turn to glass. Right then, underneath the table at this cute coffee shop in downtown Roanoke, my pinky toe is buddy-wrapped to its neighbor and my foot cushioned by an orthopedic shoe. Mom says I should get a bone-density scan, but I guess I'm too afraid to see the results. I picture an X-ray depicting a faint skeleton comprising translucent outlines. I imagine muscles and flesh are the only cushioning that protects hundreds of fragile ornaments rattling inside of me.

III.

I came out as trans on a mountainside in Craig County.

I camp on Liza's land in Meadows of Dan. Nearby cows, fences, and confederate flags tell stories that I don't fully understand. Liza has the most luscious eyes. They lay in the wet grass like a gnarled tree bent into shape by years of mountain winds. There have been several tornado warnings lately. We discuss whether foxes are a type of cat or a dog.

When I was twenty, I asked Wayne, the old man at the farmers' market in upstate New York, if I could work for him. On the first day I picked wax beans with snot droplets on my upper lip, ragweed raging in my eyes. I pitched a tent in Wayne's woods and heard the dogs howl in the highlands. Having barely slept, my face puffy, I sat on Wayne's porch at sunrise. He talked to me about what farming is really like and sent me home.

I'm at a summer party at Liza's. At dusk, there are floral dresses tinged with wood smoke, vegan slaws and doughnuts, cars angled in the grass, disparate dogs running as a pack. We synchronize our yogic breathing in the barn to the rippling thunder, the wind sneaking through the wooden boards rattling crisp dried flowers, our hands and feet covered in dust, your body breathing next to mine.

Rural spaces are loved by queer people. T Fleischmann writes of a queer haven in rural Tennessee. Eli Clare writes of coastal Oregon as a lost homeland. Some of the folks here met at a Radical Faerie commune in Tennessee. Lesbians in the 1980s held feminist retreats just on the other side of this county. Queers are making and remaking things here: flowers, food, gender, music, sex—growing new meaning out of tired soil.

I am tired of moving my body into and out of apartments. I feel like a cicada shedding its skin. As I pack my papers into cardboard boxes, I also pack fat onto my chest, hips and butt. I shred old documents; I shred muscle mass. I polish the bathroom tiles; my cheeks glisten with a pale estrogen glow.

I was leaving an apartment where the guy upstairs never wore a shirt and screamed at his girlfriend and threw things around the house and always referred to me as a man although I was not a man. The ceiling collapsed upon my guest bed, then it collapsed in my bedroom. The neighborhood cat broke into the apartment and shit on my rug. But that was also where I first kissed someone as a not-man, where I was fucked for the first time as a not-man. It is where I woke from a dream and knew that I was to become a woman. It is where I first secretly put on women's clothes that I purchased online and looked at myself in the mirror in a new dress, and I masturbated. Autogynephilia be damned, I was becoming. I was an archaeologist. I unearthed myself.

IV.
I bought the house. The house that my ex lived in when we fell in love. And the deed—a legal document affirming my ownership over a small parcel of land in this city—lists me as a "single woman."

I know that ownership is temporary and troubled, that it is backed by the power of the pen and the gun. I know that I do not really own this unceded land where Tutelo and other peoples for thousands of years have lived, that my settler colonial tenancy is simultaneously both momentary and a continuation of centuries of horrible violence. I know that this house was built at the height of Jim Crow in an all-white part of Roanoke, in a neighborhood that was not redlined and that is not yet desegregated. I know that homeownership is the path to wealth in our capitalist society and that I'm only on that path because of my racial and class privileges. That despite being a trans woman in just the second year of legal housing protections in Virginia for LGBTQIA2S+ people, my ownership in this land still bucks the trend of what most queer and trans people, especially queer and trans women, can achieve. I know what Marx said about private property. I know that property is power.

Yet here I am on my back porch under a canopy of gorgeous sunlit elderly trees. And there is June running free and exploring and smelling and she's happy and I love her, and I feel like I have done a good thing, a very monumental thing as her mother. And I remember sitting on this porch nearly five years ago and talking with loved ones who lived here about the gay bar—the first in Southwest Virginia—that opened on the adjacent parcel in 1953. And I'm going to hang Molly's roadkill bone mobile in the front window, in the same room where she made it. And we're going to grow food here and flowers and throw parties and make queer space and love one another. I'll call it Kinship House.

V.

the body is a miracle / bone on bone / flesh stretched / fat falls flabby / empty follicles once filled with hair / immunotherapy / melting blue pills / pox scars / beauty marks / my areolas / yellowing teeth / collarbone / blood and guts / this vessel / I want to be touched / I touch myself / trace bones with fingertips / cup small breasts / kiss me behind my ear / synchronize breath

Hannah is ripping up the yard at Kinship House, replacing it with vegetable stalks and flowers. I bake vegan cakes in the gas oven. A lover smooches me on the porch swing. I love the clinking sound ice cubes make when bumping in a glass of iced tea.

I underestimated how powerful it would feel to build a home, to make family with other queer women, to care for my puppy and my plants, to feed ourselves from our garden, to make music with mandolin, flute and drum, to look out upon the megachurch, the rotting wooden boards, the cornflower, the stray cat, and feel right where I belong.

Lauren Garretson-Atkinson

An Inheritance

"I think I know why Cindy's been sniffing you so much lately," my mama says to an eleven-year-old me.

We are sitting inside the ancient gray whale, a 1981 Crown Victoria, in the McCoy's parking lot while we eat gas station pizza. I stop cold when she says this, pepperoni and mushroom swirling steam against my lips. My stomach ties a knot as I remember the numerous times our dog has greeted me by forcefully pressing her boxy, muscular head between my thighs and sniffing like she's racing to solve the world's greatest mystery. Some witnessing it would laugh, others would graciously turn away, and each time I would haul my legs shut and shove her dumb face away from the direction of my greatest mortification.

I've begun to wonder if I really am dirty, like the girls at school whisper when I pass them by in fossilized corduroy jackets from the church donation center (always smelling like mothballs) and Family Dollar jeans that are cut all wrong. I worry that I'm going to be the next Kendra Loudermilk, the girl everyone's nicknamed "Tuna Fish" in commemoration of the supposed smell that seeps out from between her legs. Other than Kendra, I'm already the only other Black girl in Pocahontas County—is it possible I have *this* in common with her, too? The thought makes me want to rip my eyebrows out.

This must be why my mom's tone is so low and serious, like it gets when she is about to give me important instructions that I must not forget. She thoughtfully chews another bite and looks over at me from the driver's seat. She combs through my expression, wondering whether I am ready for her input or am in one of my "moods." I am not, and *now* I am.

"I think it's because you're getting ready to start your period," she sets the news down gingerly so that I may inspect it.

I think back to the discharge that stained my underwear a few nights before: viscid, white, and accusatory in its nature. Is that what that was?

My cheeks are suddenly hot. A beat exchanges between us—she is waiting for me to say something; I am waiting to open the car door and heave the contents of my stomach out onto the asphalt. The pizza goes rancid in my mouth, and I never want to eat mushrooms again.

"You are about to become a woman."

My mom says this carefully, like she is preparing to pass me down a family heirloom that we both know I cannot refuse. I want to tell her to keep it. I want to tell her that I am not ready to become a woman. I am not ready to put things like tampons and dicks inside of me. I am not ready to be devoured by the wolves who say I look sixteen and touch me like I am twenty. I am not ready to be told that I asked for it; not ready for blood to spill from my body like spit and piss and fear and shit and shame and tears and—

Instead, I swallow past the lump in my throat, feel my head pulled to a nod by the gravity of the moment. I break our stare after a while and drag my gaze to the passenger window. A towheaded boy runs circles around his mother's legs while she talks to Ronnie, who sleeps out on the bench next to the gas pumps on days when the older ladies work (they slip him Marlboros and Budweisers when Mr. McCoy isn't in). Ronnie says something that makes the woman's gravel-laugh pebble at my window, and the red on his face deepen. Ronnie pulls himself upright, sets his paper bag down next to him and reaches into his weathered Carhartt to offer the woman a cigarette. She lights it, looks up at the sky, blows out smoke.

When my mom asks me why I've stopped eating, I say I'm not hungry—it is only half a lie. I turn away from her and change the subject to something that will make us both forget this moment. She relents, and we do not speak of it again for a long time. Like my mama and her mama and her mama's mama before her, I leave the less pleasant things unsaid.

After all, isn't that what women do?

Pumpkin Starr

4 lil poems on 4 big feelins

1. divine isolation

rivers & voids
made whats here.
im so small innit.

one speck a grit
morphed by absence.
im one dem

rock babies.
lodged in place
tethered to sacrifice

in this loneliness, im still
a gem. unseen,
i lived, hunny.

2. ecological grief

here
    clockwork
    heat
    rain

here
    in an oven
    romanticized by perfume
    from outta season blooms.
here
    in its rotten sweet weight
    mentholated air that squeezes my napp to dread.
here
    to surrender
    to what pressure can do
    for the sky & to its people.
here
    with it all
    makes an equinox
    hard to believe.
here
    is fantastical
    when you balance
    on a cliff for so long.

3. *seasonally affected*

slowing
thoughts
another
season
of soil.

im sunken.
muscles
atrophied
kneeling
to caverns

of dirt
swaddling
what promises

to return
& what never will:

graves & gardens.

4. requited self-love

my body is no longer
forgettable. a true commitment, i no longer want to be
an orb of light.

D. Stump

Prayers to a Greater Belonging

The stretch of land where the Mountain Parkway opens up in greeting to the beginnings of mountains in eastern Kentucky is always within my mind's reach. These days, I find myself longing to remember the very first time I saw the Appalachian Mountains, and even though those distinctive first memories still hold themselves golden in my heart, now there are layers upon layers of emotions that flood my mind whenever I turn back to that parkway, just as gently as hills fold themselves into mountains.

The mouth of the Mountain Parkway guides me directly to the heart of Prestonsburg, there where the soil and air hold themselves in knowing power—they belong to the mountains and the trees, just as the mountains and trees belong to them, there where no human can pretend otherwise, no matter how hard one tries.

The humans, although they belong, too, to their terrestrial kin, also belong to Double Kwik, Food City, and the Peking Chinese Buffet. The first time my partner invited me to visit his hometown, in my well-intended attempt to win over the hearts of his family, I decided I would be the most beautiful NDN Prestonsburg had ever seen. The eyes of strangers desperately attempted to decide what to make of my queer, NDN body as we wandered through Food City. Glances and double-takes in the city always stung my skin, hot metal and piercing knives seeking to carve the whole of me into something digestible. There, in a place I had never been, a place I may have once visited only in unknowing dreams, I found myself reveling in the perception of myself held in the eyes of strangers. It was not quite acceptance I saw looking back at me, but it was not dissection or fear either. It was a curiosity, a wondering of where I could have come from, where it was I was going, who it was who had brought me here. It was in these glances, in that small moment hunting for boxes of Jiffy and canned corn, that I felt beautiful, that I felt powerful—that I first felt strangely at home in a land I had never known.

The curiosity of strangers at the presence of an obvious outsider called to me in a way I had not felt since leaving the Rez. Everyone knows everyone's business. Everyone knows everyone's family. You will spend an hour more than expected at the grocery store catching up with cousins and great-aunties, as you fail to hide your face fast enough to escape their conversation. When you hear sirens down the street, you call your mother to know who got into what kind of trouble. When you find yourself dying of boredom, you find the same people you've found your whole life, and you shoot the shit over bonfires in the middle of a familiar nowhere. Prestonsburg could not pull the wool over my eyes—despite the lack of NDNs and treaty rights, it was just an echo of a reservation, tucked into hollers and coal tipples. The lines in the sand that I had drawn in my own mind between Natives and non-Natives didn't seem as deep as I had once believed.

*

As I do whenever I meet a new corner of the Earth, that first evening in Prestonsburg, I sat outside my partner's mamaw's trailer and offered tobacco to the world around me. Although I had weaned myself off the recreational use of cigarettes by then, shifting instead to a spiritual approach to smoking, I thanked the tobacco for the familiar burning in my lungs. Tobacco had carried me through mountains of hardships over the years, and then, there I was, carrying this medicine back to the mountains.

Otsadadolisdiha. Galvlohi ginidoda, nvda ginilisi, elohihno ginetsi—galieliga, sginigeyuha, otsaliheliga.

Although simple, the Earth, I believe, remembered my prayers. She remembered the laying down of tobacco to listen to the clouds of smoke and breath that carried my words to where they belonged, to greet me back in Her own laughter and warmth. This remembrance, I knew, should not have been a surprise. It is the way it has been for as long as my people can remember, and even longer still. The Earth has not forgotten Her duties, Her responsibilities, nor has She forgotten what She is due, nor our responsibilities as Her children. I wanted to believe, deep in my bones, that someone, somewhere among these mountains, still put down tobacco in prayer. No matter what language they would use, or how long they had been trying, I wanted to believe the Earth would greet them as She had me.

My prayer was not offered from myself alone—*ginidoda, ginilisi, ginetsi,* these are all said in plurals, our grandfather, our grandmother, our mother. It is the way I had always been told to pray. Even when I was alone with my pack of cigarettes, sometimes sitting among the grasses, other times flicking ash out my car window, I always put these words into plurals, as I never want to believe that I walk without my kin, that when I give thanks, I am not giving thanks alone. In Kanien'kéha, the so-called Mohawk language, prayers are started with *akwé:kon énska entitewahwe'nón:ni nonkwa'nikòn:ra*, all together as one, we wrap it up in our minds. In that prayer, and in my Tsalagi prayer, there is an innate need for community, an unbreakable responsibility to speak as one in thanks to the Earth, because She takes care of us all.

As I sat there in a town that I was learning to fit into its own place in my life, I suddenly was unable to escape an avalanche of questions. Who here was speaking with me, to give thanks to *our* grandmother the moon and *our* mother the Earth? What community backed me in my responsibility to the Earth, and who here could I be responsible to?

I was deeply thankful and humbled, will always be, by how quickly my partner's kin accepted me into the fabric of their lives and kinship. I am thankful for how they care for me as an autonomous human being, my own person, and see in me an importance that stretches beyond the deep love I hold for this human they also called kin. When I raise up my prayers of gratitude, this newfound kin most certainly have their place in my words. I feel myself tied to them in this web of kinship that holds me responsible to those I love, a web that wraps me in their own loving protection and grace. In that moment on the mountainside, my heart was full of their love and acceptance, but there still remained a part of me in the shadows, hungry and touch-starved, that longed for something else.

There is a painful reminder here, and at first I didn't understand why, of the family that I had to leave behind if I were to embrace all the queerness within me. In Tsalagi, we Indigiqueer kin can call ourselves "strange hearted," and I embrace the truth that no matter where I go in this life, I have always felt strange. Never, however, have I wanted to be a stranger—the stranger I became and remained for many years of my life, to my Anitsalagi kin. Disconnection comes from many places, through traumas that happen both before and long after we leave the safety of the womb, and I have borne the scars of both for as long as I can remember.

I grew up hearing of the forced removal of the Anitsalagi branch of my family, how our kin were taken away from the mountains and marshes of the Southeast and placed in the traditional lands of other peoples—how that removal scattered my family like wild seeds, left to grow in strange and infertile lands. We did grow, however, into our own thick groves and patches of wildflowers. There was no predicting where we could call home.

Learning to call Kentucky home, discovering the web of kinship established here as part of my family searched for more gentle land than that which was allotted in Oklahoma, has come with a steep price; it has given me wounds that I am still learning to unravel. Non-Natives often do not afford Natives the reality of being messy, of having complex and complicated relationships with our communities—we are expected to be constantly in harmony, constantly in balance, and consistently simple and humble beings. The truth of the matter is that we are humans, like any other, who can make mistakes, cause harm, and mistreat our kin.

My queerness, in many instances, has not been nurtured, it has not been held fondly and respectfully by all of my kin in the way it deserves. I have often come back to this truth, wondering how to simultaneously carry the responsibilities I hold to my kin and communities, while the weight of queerphobia pulls so heavily at my neck. The rift between longing to belong to my Anitsalagi kin and the wounds I must soothe from the same kin who are supposed to care for me in turn has led me to many distant and cold places, in myself and in this state I have sometimes reluctantly come to cherish. If being NDN means being in relation with those who claim you, what then, can become of an NDN whose kin has failed to live in loving relations, to claim the whole of your being without shame and bigotry?

When I sit in those hills that grow into mountains, I hold the sorrow for the parts of my family I only have in fractions and half-truths. I sit in the worth of my own queerness, and in anger at how some of those who claim to love me have worked to destroy it. Sometimes, in a quiet voice, too timid to shout, I plead to the beings that surround me to mother the child within that longs for belonging.

This is when I turn to the stories that have been given to me, the words passed from mouth, to hand, to ear, to blood. I remember the stories of giants that protect the mountains, the little people who dance around tree stumps, the spider who carried drops of the sun down to The People. I remember stories of ancestors who fled to the loving arms of these same sprawling mountains to escape colonial brutality. I remember that my people have loved, cared for, and stood in awe at the beauty of these mountains, and that the mountains, in turn, have loved and cared for them. I may have become a stranger to my Anitsalagi family, but I am no stranger to my ancestors, and I am certainly no stranger to these mountains.

I remember, too, fondly and with humility, that the very grass that embraces me, the branches that fold and crisscross above me, the sun that rains down its golden light, are all my kin. It is the responsibility to protect, to provide, to shelter and feed, to give thanks, and ask for what we need that binds us to one another. I am the protector and the protected—this, too, makes us family.

Being Two-Spirit, as its meaning sits within my own heart, has always called me to be a bridge, to open myself to the flow of all things that move between, from within and without myself. This Two-Spirit body, *hia asegi aquadanvdo*—this strange heart, bears witness to all the ways the past bleeds into the present, circles back into the future, how time kisses itself on the cheeks and holds its own hands, as those before us who once walked the Earth and shared in these human responsibilities now walk within our blood. NDN time says there is no past, no future, just a series of now-and-thens, a long line of presents that fold into tomorrows and bleed yesterdays. Time is immortal, never ending; it moves through us in ways we can only feel in the changing of our skin and the growing of our nails. Time, in all of its might, is also our kin, as it brings us to the feet of our ancestors and descendants until we come full circle with all that was and will be.

The way my family tells the story of our ancestors before the Trail of Tears, my Cherokee kin called what is now considered Northern Georgia and North Carolina home. In its own right, the encroaching presence of larger and larger settler communities was also its own forced removal as the livelihoods and ways of being of our kin were disrupted, shamed, and ostracized. The southern stretch of the Appalachian Mountains that already held its arms open in protection and safety called out to my kin, beckoning them to go deeper, to envelop themselves in the security only the mountains could shelter. The mountains guided them northward, through thickets and valleys, until they could take root in a place beyond settler time, nurtured by fertile land and the restful silence of peace.

My kin never divided the land between the Virginias and Kentucky in their minds or words, so the exact location they called home may never be revealed to me. I, however, have not only found peace with the unknown but have found myself beginning to revel in the fluidity and mystery of exactly where they laid their heads to rest in these mountains. It allows me to embrace the fullness of their world, unconcerned with state boundaries and the ever-pressing forward motion of settler time. I call out to the mountains and feel their immensity surround me, and I bow my head in acceptance of a power much greater than I could ever summon alone.

I would never say that I am culturally, politically, or socially Appalachian, as I have come to respect, advocate for, and listen to the people who own that belonging in their own right. I would not even consider myself to be of Appalachian descent, as that carries its own social implications. I would consider myself, in part, a gift from these mountains' foster children—the ones they protected with solace and generosity. There is a complex, winding sense of belonging that has kept me gun-shy and mildly confused, in ways that I have come to understand as one of the many ways we as Indigenous people have come to reclaim our kinship with the land—the divide between what it is, has become, what it has been, and all that it will forever be.

I am a child of these mountains just the same as I am a child of the Great Lakes, as I am a child of Oklahoma, as I am a child of corn stalks and sweet grass baskets. Belonging is not divisible, we are not fractions of all and whom we have come from, but an agglomeration, a weaving of verse and music whose notes are not yet finished being written. In the beautiful, strange, messy ways I have learned to belong to people and pieces of the land, standing in front of those mountains, feeling the waves of stories rolling through me both from and beyond my own kin, I have begun to learn the missing piece to my own puzzle that has taken over twenty years to fathom:

I, too, can belong to myself.

*

Coming back to this piece nearly half a year after I wrote it has met me with a stirring whirlpool of emotions that I can only try to name here—grief, fear, longing, compassion. My grief for the relationship that (re)introduced me to Appalachia that ended since I had originally completed this piece lives here in these words, and I try to extend to my past self, who had so much faith and trust in that love, all my compassion and softness.

There was fear to return to this piece, fear that it would no longer fit into the truth that it once called appropriate, that it once called home in my heart, now that I am no longer with the partner who was so present in this writing. I feared what emotions and homesickness rereading this piece could elicit in my strange heart, and in its folds, I have truly found that "homesickness" is the champion of all my big and sprawling emotions.

As I sit here listening to Tyler Childers, writing this addendum to a piece I thought I had completed months ago, I realize how deeply I have been grieving Eastern Kentucky in my life since leaving my former partner. Knowing someone's hometown like the back of your hand is its own love language. Me being the type of human I am that forms such deep bonds with the spirit of the places that hold me in their arms, I long for the land in the same way I long for human life. I am jealous of the places in this world I will never see, or that I have longed to see, like a jealous lover.

I miss Appalachia, in all my honest truth, more than I miss that relationship. My most immediate reaction to leaving that partner was a sinking feeling of losing a deep kinship to Appalachia, not only the land but the music, the food, the festivals, the smells, and changing of the seasons painted on mountainsides. I comforted myself many-a-night by knowing that this pain is not foreign to me, at least not to my blood, as I know my family must have felt ripped from their mountain homes. Every year on September 10, which passed only a couple weeks before writing these words, I sit with the truth of their 1838 removal from what is known to us as *Tsalaguwet, Old Cherokee* (what is known to settlers as North Carolina).

This year, my remembrance of the 1838 removal sat closer to me than my own skin as I mourned the past relationship with Appalachia that I now must leave behind, a second loss of home that I never would have imagined for myself. It was in this mourning, however, that I realized Appalachia is not gone to me. The romantic relationships we form with human kin are not the lifeblood threads of attachment that Western culture wants them to be, they do not color our life with meaning; even the relations that we form through that own bond of kinship still exist for ourselves.

The ancestors, including those trees and hills and mountains and rivers that live in our bones, have strange and beautiful ways of calling to us, in places we never would have expected. Appalachia found me again on its own turning and winding road, and in shedding the weight of that former partnership, I have freed myself to exploring a world in my own way, without having to fit into someone else's framework of kinship. I still have many other friendships and connections to Appalachia that nurture me, that receive me in reciprocity, that hold me in loving ways beyond my little human understanding of the web of connection and nourishment that surrounds us.

We find meaning in all the places meaning calls to us. We find home in all the places that invite us to sit at the table and eat. We find love in all the words that live under our skin, asking us gently to allow ourselves, to give, to receive, to live in softness and responsibility to all of creation.

*

Gadohno usdi tsayolega, nasgi nigalsdodi nigadi elohi tsidetsayosga?
What are the things you seek, since you leave all the world to find them?

Brandon Sun Eagle Jent

this world loves me too

Overcome with love for all that lives, I open
a human heart-shaped door and try to push
the land inside me: press, roll, squeeze,
tug. It won't budge. So I just leave
the door wide open,
                              a guest invited
in tastes and whiffs, breaths and blinks,
my chest a keyhole, this sunlit world
a ballerina in a jewel-encrusted music box,
each rotation a moving picture.

I watch you build your houses, embrace
your families, I wave hello from my heart's chambers
while you take your evening walks, four seasons
coating each curve of my soul's dwelling place
like weathered wallpaper:

October's crackling confetti,
oxblood and burnt sienna;

January's sharp icicles
and powdered snow;

April's sweet memories
tucked in honeysuckle lockets;

July's sermon,
humid air pressing mountains
like dried flowers, prayers between pages.

Barn swallows build nests atop serpentine
vines, a dry-rotted doorframe reincarnated
in kudzu. The sky blooms a bouquet of flame
azaleas, daylilies, ironweed, soft petals
of light trailing across the mossy floor.

Night swallows the horizon, time washing
in like tides until there's no room, no door,
no you or me, just an earthen ouroboros
swirling in on itself, a snow globe shaken
by celestial hands, lightning bug glitter
flashing green along the glass and flitting
in and out of this fist-sized secret garden
that remembers   remembers that this wild
thing, this speck of universe is a vessel
forever burbling, bubbling
                                      with love.

Acknowledgments

First and foremost, thank you to each of the contributors for sharing such vulnerable and powerful pieces with the world and for agreeing to be part of this collection. Thank you Carter Sickels, Joy Cedar, Brandon Sun Eagle Jent, Rayna Momen, Lucien Darjeun Meadows, hermelinda cortés, Joe Tolbert Jr., Jai Arun Ravine, G. Samantha Rosenthal, Lauren Garretson-Atkinson, Pumpkin Starr, and D. Stump. Second, infinite thanks to Abby Freeland for your patience, support, co-thinking, and encouragement over the years it took for this collection to come together. It was delightful to work with you on this project.

Thank you to everyone at the University Press of Kentucky who worked behind the scenes to make this book a physical reality, from peer review to copyedits to cover design and beyond. Thank you to the team behind the Appalachian Futures series for creating such a necessary space within regional publishing and for welcoming this little collection into your fold.

Thank you to the extended Appalachian Writers' Workshop community and network, especially those I've had the pleasure of meeting and connecting with at Hindman Settlement School over the years. That was the first writing space where I found encouragement and inspiration that made me wonder if maybe I, too, could someday write books. I'll never forget Marianne Worthington finding me after the first time I read at the workshop in the summer of 2013. I was so nervous I could hardly function, but Marianne approached me right away, asked me to submit the story to *Still: The Journal*, and took me under her wing for the evening. I doubt I ever would have submitted to a journal without that encouragement. Thank you, Marianne. Thanks also to so many other wonderful writers I've met, taken classes with, been inspired by, and learned from through that network, including but not limited to (with apologies to any I forgot to mention) Silas House, Jason Howard, Robert Gipe, Carter Sickels, Fenton Johnson, Rebecca Gayle Howell, Neema Avashia, and many more.

Thank you to my early STAY Project crew, my BAM fam, and all the Appalachian organizers, radicals, queers, and artists whose existence inspires me and whose work motivates me to continue working in and with stories that, hopefully, help carve out a little more space for our people and places to be.

Thanks, finally, to these mountains—for loving us so generously and patiently, despite and in spite of ourselves.

Contributors

Joy Cedar (she/they) is a Two-Spirited poet, community worker, and visual artist. She incorporates survivance into the heart of her work. They live in Kentucky with their dog.

hermelinda cortés (she/they) schemes and daydreams about how to use organizing, narrative, and strategic communications to build power, fortify lasting connections between communities, dismantle systems of domination, and build the liberated world we and future generations deserve. The child of Mexicans and West Virginians, country folks, farmers, factory workers, and trailer parks, she has dedicated her life to the journey of liberation and to the work of social movements for the last fifteen years. hermelinda is a writer, curandera in training, organizer, communicator, and strategist. She lives in the Shenandoah Valley of Virginia where she writes, cooks, grows flowers, and raises her kid in the company of dogs and chickens. She believes in the magic, alchemy, and revolutionary possibilities of small towns and rural people.

Lauren Garretson-Atkinson (she/her) grew up in the mountains of rural West Virginia. She is a Kimbilio Fiction Fellow and holds an MFA in fiction from Virginia Tech. Her work can be found in *Open Minds Quarterly* and *Joyland Magazine*.

Rae Garringer (they/them) is a writer, oral historian, and audio producer who grew up on a sheep farm in southeastern West Virginia and now lives a few counties away on S'atsoyaha and S̆aawanwaki lands. Rae is the founder of Country Queers, a multimedia community-based oral history project documenting rural and small-town LGBTQIA2S+ experiences since 2013. They are the author of *Country Queers: A Love Letter*, published in October 2024.

Brandon Sun Eagle Jent (he/she/they) resides in Eastern Kentucky on the unceded lands of the ᎠᏂᏴᏫᏯ, S'atsoyaha, and Shawanwaki nations. A lover of words, languages, and stories, he holds a master's degree in linguistic theory and typology from the University of Kentucky. Brandon writes poetry as part of a lifelong dialogue between herself, their kin (human and more-than-human), and the natural world, making each piece both a transcript and a love letter.

Lucien Darjeun Meadows (he/him) was born in Virginia and raised in West Virginia. Lucien has received fellowships and awards from the Academy of American Poets, American Alliance of Museums, and National Association for Interpretation. His debut poetry collection, *In the Hands of the River*, was published in 2022.

Rayna Momen (they/them) holds a PhD in sociology. They are a Black, nonbinary poet, queer criminologist, and abolitionist born and raised in West Virginia. Momen cofounded a higher-education-in-prison initiative that expands educational access for currently and formerly incarcerated people. They found their purpose building community inside and outside of prison walls as a means of dismantling oppressive systems.

Jai Arun Ravine (they/them) is the author of แล้ว *and then entwine: lesson plans, poems, knots*, a book that reimagines immigration history and attempts to transform cultural inheritances of silence. Their short film *Tom / Trans / Thai* approaches the silence around female-to-male transgender identity in the Thai context and has screened internationally. The film's companion scholarly article, "*Toms* and Zees: Locating FTM Identity in Thailand," was published in *Transgender Studies Quarterly* 1(3). Their second book, *The Romance of Siam: A Pocket Guide*, is a subverted travel guide that consumes and regurgitates orientalism, the tourist archive, and white desire. They live in West Virginia.

G. Samantha Rosenthal (she/her) is an associate professor of history at Roanoke College in Salem, Virginia, and a visiting assistant professor of American history at Washington and Lee University in Lexington, Virginia. She is the author of two books, most recently *Living Queer History: Remembrance and Belonging in a Southern City*. She is the cofounder of the Southwest Virginia LGBTQ+ History Project, a nationally recognized queer public history initiative. Her work has received recognition from the National Council on Public History, the Oral History Association, the Committee on LGBT History, the American Society for Environmental History, and the Working-Class Studies Association.

Pumpkin Starr (they/them) is a creative from north Alabama.

D. Stump (they/them) is a Two-Spirit Atsalag and Kanien'kehá:ka member of the Long Hair Clan and Wolf Clan, respectively. They live currently on occupied and unceded Shaawanowi and Anitsalagi land in Gvnvdvgi. They balance their time between making coffee, playing with their cat, studying language revitalization, and striving to be in good relation with all their kin that surround them.

Joe Tolbert Jr. (he/him) is a writer and cultural organizer who works at the intersections of art and culture, spirituality, and collective liberation. He received his BS in communications from the University of Tennessee, Knoxville, and completed his MDiv in social ethics from Union Theological Seminary in the City of New York. He is a sought-after facilitator, creative producer, and cultural strategist who works with communities and arts institutions to help them harness the power of art and culture through his company, Art at the Intersections.

APPALACHIAN FUTURES
Black, Native, and Queer Voices

SERIES EDITORS: Annette Saunooke Clapsaddle, Davis Shoulders, and Crystal Wilkinson

This book series gives voice to Black, Native, Latinx, Asian, Queer, and other nonwhite or ignored identities within the Appalachian region.

Black Freedom Struggle in Urban Appalachia
Edited by J. Z. Bennett, Christy L. McGuire, Lori Delale-O'Connor, T. Elon Dancy II, and Sabina Vaught

Affrilachia: Testimonies
Chris Aluka Berry with Kelly Elaine Navies and Maia A. Surdam

No Son of Mine: A Memoir
Jonathan Corcoran

To Belong Here: A New Generation of Queer, Trans, and Two-Spirit Appalachian Writers
Edited by Rae Garringer

Tar Hollow Trans: Essays
Stacy Jane Grover

Deviant Hollers: Queering Appalachian Ecologies for a Sustainable Future
Edited by Zane McNeill and Rebecca Scott

Reading, Writing, and Queer Survival: Affects, Matterings, and Literacies across Appalachia
Caleb Pendygraft

Appalachian Ghost: A Photographic Reimagining of the Hawk's Nest Tunnel Disaster
Raymond Thompson Jr.